At Issue

Is Selling
Body Parts Ethical?

Other Books in the At Issue Series:

At Issue

Is Selling Body Parts Ethical?

Christina Fisanick, Book Editor

GREENHAVEN PRESS
A part of Gale, Cengage Learning

GALE
CENGAGE Learning™

Detroit • New York • San Francisco • New Haven, Conn • Waterville, Maine • London

Christine Nasso, *Publisher*
Elizabeth Des Chenes, *Managing Editor*

© 2010 Greenhaven Press, a part of Gale, Cengage Learning.

Gale and Greenhaven Press are registered trademarks used herein under license.

For more information, contact:
Greenhaven Press
27500 Drake Rd.
Farmington Hills, MI 48331-3535
Or you can visit our Internet site at gale.cengage.com

For product information and technology assistance, contact us at

Gale Customer Support, 1-800-877-4253
For permission to use material from this text or product, submit all requests online at www.cengage.com/permissions

Further permissions questions can be emailed to permissionrequest@cengage.com

Articles in Greenhaven Press anthologies are often edited for length to meet page requirements. In addition, original titles of these works are changed to clearly present the main thesis and to explicitly indicate the author's opinion. Every effort is made to ensure that Greenhaven Press accurately reflects the original intent of the authors. Every effort has been made to trace the owners of copyrighted material.

Cover image © Images.com/Corbis.

LIBRARY OF CONGRESS CATALOGING-IN-PUBLICATION DATA

Is selling body parts ethical? / Christina Fisanick, book editor.
    p. cm. -- (At issue)
   Includes bibliographical references and index.
   ISBN 978-0-7377-4306-7 (hardcover)
   ISBN 978-0-7377-4305-0 (pbk.)
   1. Donation of organs, tissues, etc--Moral and ethical aspects. I. Fisanick, Christina.
   RD129.5.I8 2009
   174.2'97954--dc22

                                       2009020986

Printed in the United States of America
1 2 3 4 5 6 7 13 12 11 10 09

Contents

Introduction

In response to a growing world market for human organs, the United States government passed the National Organ Transplant Act in 1984, which made it illegal "for any person to knowingly acquire, receive, or otherwise transfer any human organ for valuable consideration for use in human transplantation if the transfer affects interstate commerce." Enacted out of concern for the well-being of those people who potentially could be exploited by organ brokers, the government's restriction has led some citizens, especially patients in need of organs, to question this policy on the basis of human rights. The issue is further complicated by the fact that replenishable body products, such as reproductive goods, can be sold. Why, some have wondered, is it illegal to sell livers and kidneys but not sperm and eggs?

In 1980 the United States Supreme Court took up this very question in *Diamond v. Chakrabarty*. The justices ruled that human-made products, such as hair, bacteria, and urine, were considered patentable because a new organism was created that had "markedly different characteristics from any found in nature." This landmark ruling paved the way for the sale of human byproducts, which include sperm and eggs. Since then, people in need of such products have found ways of using the case to justify their trade. In the case of human eggs, for example, women are paid not for the eggs they produce but for the harvesting procedure itself.

Fertility clinics and sperm and egg donors justify the payment for their services by pointing to what egg donation and surrogacy attorney Tom Pinkerton has referred to as "personal procreative liberty." Like those who argue in favor of compensating organ donors, Pinkerton believes that men and women have the right to be paid for the risk to their health and for their body products. After all, he argues, "What is the harm?

We want to treat the donors with respect." A woman releases eggs each month; therefore, her health and future well-being are compromised only during retrieval.

Not everyone agrees with Pinkerton. George Annas of the American Society for Reproductive Medicine asserts that while sperm and hair do grow back, a woman does not have an endless reservoir of eggs, and the procedure is painful and potentially harmful to the donor. He wants the selling of eggs to be made illegal because "it is a procedure that puts women at risk, risk of various diseases and possibly the risk of infertility itself." He thinks that the practice should be outlawed, but in the absence of such a policy, he urges that women be compensated only for the pain and risk of the procedure and not for the egg itself.

Although a 2007 article in the journal *Fertility and Sterility* reported that the national average compensation for egg donors is $4,217, the trend seems to edge toward higher compensation to ensure the best-quality eggs and to guarantee that a donor will be found. In a *New York Times* article about the recent surge in demand for human eggs, donor Samantha Carolan states that "I don't think I would have done it without compensation." Her resistance is echoed in the concerns of would-be parents who argue that without payment, there will be a considerable shortage of viable eggs, which is evidenced by the current crisis in the United Kingdom, where it is illegal to pay sperm and egg donors.

Critics of compensation for egg donation worry that the money may cloud the judgment of donors, who are often young women in need of money. These concerns are in response to several recent instances in which couples have offered up to $100,000 to viable egg donors from elite universities. Even among supporters of donor compensation, such figures seem troubling. Josephine Johnston, an associate for law and bioethics at the Hastings Center, is not opposed to paying egg donors, but is concerned about what she sees as excessive compensation. She wonders, "How much is that person actually giving informed consent about the medical procedure and really listening and thinking as it's being described and its risks are explained?" In other words, these young women may be blinded by getting out of debt or paying for graduate school and not thinking about their future reproduction possibilities and the toll the actual procedure will take on their health.

Although some states have attempted to ban the sale of sperm and eggs, the practice remains legal in the United States, which confounds some patients in need of life-saving transplants. Why, they wonder, is it legal to sell body products like sperm and eggs and not an extra kidney or lung? After all, the ethical dilemmas are the same. The poor are just as exploited in the exchange of reproductive products for money as they would be for other body parts. And the dangers to the donor are just as real for egg donation as they are for organ donation. Even some physicians, such as Eli Friedman of the State University of New York and Amy Friedman of Yale University, have joined this side of the debate, contending that a well-regulated market for organ donation "could save thousands of lives each year."

A clear resolution to this difficult situation is unlikely to be achieved anytime soon. As people live longer than ever before, the need for human organs will continue to climb. The same is true of sperm and eggs, given that couples wait longer to begin a family. Arguments about the complexities of compensating donors, such as those discussed by the authors in *At Issue: Is Selling Body Parts Ethical?*, will surely continue well into the next several decades as the potential for manufacturing body parts and cloning human beings becomes more likely. Until then, those in need and those who want to provide must find ways to help each other that are legal, ethical, and worthwhile.

1

The Sale of Body Parts Should Be Regulated

Sam Vaknin

Sam Vaknin is a Senior Business Correspondent for United Press International.

Vaknin portrays a grim picture of the current black market trade in human body parts. Those who sell their organs are usually individuals in developing nations in extreme poverty who make very little from the sale, while those who transport the organs usually make a fortune reselling the organs to recipients in rich, developed countries. Part of the organ trade involves the abduction of individuals, including children, and the theft of their organs. Vaknin applauds the willingness of the American Medical Association to investigate "the effects [that] paying for cadaveric organs would have on the current shortage" of organs. He concludes that the current international ban on organ sales has produced the black market trade, and it would be "better to legalize and regulate the trade than transform it into a form of organized crime."

SKOPJE, Macedonia, Nov. 13 (UPI)—A kidney fetches $2,700 in Turkey. According to last month's issue of the *Journal of the American Medical Association*, this is a high price. An Indian or Iraqi kidney enriches its former owner by a mere $1,000. Wealthy clients later pay for the rare organ up to $150,000.

Two years ago, CBS News aired a documentary filmed by Antenna 3 of Spain, in which undercover reporters in Mexico were asked by a priest, acting as a middleman for a doctor, to pay close to $1 million for a single kidney. An auction of a human kidney on eBay in February 2000 drew a bid of $100,000 before the company put a stop to it. Another auction in September 1999 drew $5.7 million—though, probably, merely as a prank.

Organ harvesting operations flourish in Turkey, in Central Europe, mainly in the Czech Republic, and in the Caucasus, mostly in Georgia. They operate on Turkish, Moldovan, Russian, Ukrainian, Belarusian, Romanian, Bosnian, Kosovar, Macedonian, Albanian and assorted East European donors.

They remove kidneys, lungs, pieces of liver, even corneas, bones, tendons, heart valves, skin and other salable human bits. The organs are kept in cold storage and air lifted to illegal distribution centers in the United States, Germany, Scandinavia, the United Kingdom, Israel, South Africa, and other rich, industrialized locales. It gives "brain drain" a new, spine chilling meaning.

[Organ harvesters] remove kidneys, lungs, pieces of liver, even corneas, bones, tendons, heart valves, skin and other salable human bits. The organs are kept in cold storage and air lifted to illegal distribution centers in the United States, Germany, Scandinavia, the United Kingdom, Israel, South Africa, and other rich, industrialized locales.

Organ trafficking has become an international trade. It involves Indian, Thai, Philippine, Brazilian, Turkish and Israeli doctors who scour the Balkan and other destitute regions for tissues. The *Washington Post* reported last week that in a single village in Moldova, 14 out of 40 men were reduced by penury to selling body parts.

Last year, Moldova cut off the thriving baby adoption trade due to an—unfounded—fear the toddlers were being dissected for spare organs. According to the Israeli daily Ha'aretz, the Romanians are investigating similar allegations in Israel and have withheld permission to adopt Romanian babies from dozens of eager and out-of-pocket couples. American authorities are scrutinizing a 2-year-old Moldovan harvesting operation based in the United States.

Organ theft and trading in Ukraine is a smooth operation. According to news agencies, last August three Ukrainian doctors were charged in Lvov with trafficking in the organs of victims of road accidents. The doctors used helicopters to ferry kidneys and livers to colluding hospitals. They charged up to $19,000 per organ.

The west Australian daily surveyed in January the thriving organs business in Bosnia-Herzegovina. Sellers are offering their wares openly, through newspaper ads. Prices can reach $68,000. Compared to an average monthly wage of less than $200, this is an unimaginable fortune.

National health insurance schemes turn a blind eye. Israel participates in the costs of purchasing organs abroad, though only subject to rigorous vetting of the sources of the donation. Still, a May 2001 article in the *New York Times Magazine*, quotes "the coordinator of kidney transplantation at Hadassah University Hospital in Jerusalem (as saying that) 60 of the 244 patients currently receiving post-transplant care purchased their new kidney from a stranger—just short of 25 percent of the patients at one of Israel's largest medical centers participating in the organ business."

Many Israelis—attempting to avoid scrutiny—travel to East Europe, accompanied by Israeli doctors, to perform the transplantation surgery. These junkets are euphemistically known as "transplant tourism." Clinics have sprouted all over the benighted region. Israeli doctors have recently visited impoverished Macedonia, Bulgaria, Kosovo and Yugoslavia to discuss with local businessmen and doctors the setting up of kidney transplant clinics.

Such open involvement in what can be charitably described as a latter-day slave trade gives rise to a new wave of thinly disguised anti-Semitism. The *Ukrainian Echo*, quoting the Ukrinform news agency, Jan. 7 reported that, implausibly, a Ukrainian guest worker died in Tel-Aviv in mysterious circumstances and his heart was removed. The Interpol, according to the paper, is investigating this lurid affair.

According to scholars, reports of organ thefts and related abductions, mainly of children, have been rife in Poland and Russia at least since 1991. The buyers are supposed to be rich Arabs.

"We found in many countries—from Brazil and Argentina to India, Russia, Romania, Turkey to South Africa and parts of the United States—a kind of 'apartheid medicine' that divides the world into two distinctly different populations of 'organs suppliers' and 'organs receivers.'"

Nancy Scheper-Hughes, an anthropologist at the University of California at Berkeley and co-founder of Organs Watch, a research and documentation center, is also a member and co-author of the *Bellagio Task Force Report on Transplantation, Bodily Integrity and the International Traffic in Organs*. In a report presented in June 2001 to the House Subcommittee on International Operations and Human Rights, she substantiated at least the nationality of the alleged buyers, though not the urban legends regarding organ theft: "In the Middle East residents of the Gulf States (Kuwait, Saudi Arabia, and Oman) have for many years traveled to India, the Philippines, and to Eastern Europe to purchase kidneys made scarce locally due to local fundamentalist Islamic teachings that allow organ transplantation (to save a life), but prohibit organ harvesting from brain-dead bodies.

"Meanwhile, hundreds of kidney patients from Israel, which has its own well-developed, but under-used transplantation centers (due to ultra-orthodox Jewish reservations about brain death) travel in 'transplant tourist' junkets to Turkey, Moldova, Romania where desperate kidney sellers can be found, and to Russia where an excess of lucrative cadaveric organs are produced due to lax standards for designating brain death, and to South Africa where the amenities in transplantation clinics in private hospitals can resemble four-star hotels.

"We found in many countries—from Brazil and Argentina to India, Russia, Romania, Turkey to South Africa and parts of the United States—a kind of 'apartheid medicine' that divides the world into two distinctly different populations of 'organs suppliers' and 'organs receivers.'"

Russia, together with Estonia, China and Iraq, are, indeed, a major harvesting and trading centers. International news agencies described, two years ago, how a grandmother in Ryazan tried to sell her grandchild to a mediator. The boy was to be smuggled to the West and there dismembered for his organs. The uncle, who assisted in the matter, was supposed to collect $70,000—a fortune in Russian terms.

When confronted by the European Union on this issue, Russia responded that it lacks the resources required to monitor organ donations. The Italian magazine, *Happy Web*, reports that organ trading has taken to the Internet. A simple query on the Google search engine yields thousands of Web sites purporting to sell various body parts—mostly kidneys— for up to $125,000. The sellers are Russian, Moldovan, Ukrainian and Romanian.

Scheper-Hughes, an avid opponent of legalizing any form of trade in organs, says that "in general, the movement and flow of living donor organs—mostly kidneys—is from South to North, from poor to rich, from black and brown to white, and from female to male bodies."

Yet, this summer, bowing to reality, the American Medical Association commissioned a study to examine the effects of paying for cadaveric organs would have on the current shortage. The 1984 National Organ Transplant Act that forbids such payments is also under attack. Bills to amend it were submitted recently by several congressmen. These are steps in the right direction.

Organ trafficking is the outcome of the international ban on organ sales and live donor organs. But wherever there is demand there is a market. Excruciating poverty of potential donors, lengthening patient waiting lists and the better quality of organs harvested from live people make organ sales an irresistible proposition. The medical professions and authorities everywhere would do better to legalize and regulate the trade rather than transform it into a form of organized crime. The inhabitants of Moldova would surely appreciate it.

2

Regulated Organ Donor Markets Should Be Prohibited

Alastair V. Campbell

Alastair V. Campbell is Chen Su Lan Centennial Professor of Medical Ethics in the medical faculty of the National University of Singapore. He is the author of many articles and books, including Medicine of the Person, *which he co-edited with John Cox and Bill K.W.M. Fulford.*

Regulating the organ donor market is not a solution to the world's lack of available human organs. The basic principles behind selling organs undercut the value of charitable organ donation. After all, gifting an organ is done solely for the benefit of another and not for self gain. In addition, recent studies have shown that establishing a regulated organ market still results in the exploitation of the poor and will severely tax an already-suffering world health care system.

In the current controversy over whether an organ market should be legislated, opponents of the ban have argued that an enlightened and rational perspective would remove most, if not all, of the ethical objections.

Current international opinion, however, is unwavering in its objection to all forms of commercialisation of the procurement process. The World Health Organisation and the World Medical Association strongly oppose payment for organ donation.

Alastair V. Campbell, "No Such Thing as an Ethical Organ Market," *The Straits Times*, July 10, 2008. Reproduced by permission.

Good Reasons for Banning Organ Trading

In a recent international summit in Istanbul on Transplant Tourism and Organ Trafficking convened by the Transplantation Society and International Society of Nephrology, it was reaffirmed that the ethical basis of transplant policies and programmes should remain equitable in allocation. Their primary objective should be to promote the optimal health and well-being of donors and recipients.

These principles preclude financial considerations or material gain. The ban on organ trading is not irrational, a mere emotional response or a prejudice, but is based on good reasons.

Organ trading is wrong in principle because it presupposes that the body is a piece of property akin to our material possessions (house, car, etc). While a body part like a kidney is alienable, meaning it can be transferred to another, it is certainly not fungible (easily replaced by something similar) or commensurable (its value quantified and compared to another object).

The gift of an organ is different from selling it, since the organ is gifted out of the wish to benefit another person, not for financial gain.

Organ trading has negative social effects in that it undercuts the gift relationship between donors and recipients. Gift ethic or altruism—with its effect on social solidarity—is the rationale for many current procurement systems for cadaveric organs [those taken from the recently deceased].

If a live organ market is instituted, many people may opt out from altruistic giving—thus reducing the supply of transplantable organs. A recent study in Austria has shown that financial incentives would have this effect. Demand may also be made for certain forms of payment for cadaveric organs.

There is a strong reason for a universal ban on organ trading by all countries (except Iran). Once this barrier is breached, it is hard to justify why the law should not allow the live body trade to be extended to other "expendable" parts like hands and single eye corneas.

Furthermore, once the ban is lifted, the current organ traffickers will have the justification they need. It can be argued that a regulated market will eliminate or reduce the black market.

But so long as the national system still operates on principles of utility and equity with regard to allocation of organs—if not, perceptions of social injustice will arise—there will be perceptions of inefficiency for those on the waiting list.

So in reality, the black market will continue albeit in different forms such as offering direct higher cash payment to the vendors.

Many current poor vendors have expressed "donor regret."

Ethical Market Is Misleading

A recent review of the Iranian system in the *British Medical Journal* clearly shows that the legislation of an organ market in Iran has not corrected the problem of the black market and the exploitation of the poor as suppliers. The article also points out that the waiting list for kidneys in Iran has not been eliminated.

The notion of an "ethical and regulated market" is misleading:

One, it is inevitably exploitative, with the poor being the majority, if not all, of the vendors. Many current poor vendors have expressed "donor regret." The selling of an organ did not help them out of poverty and in fact had significant negative impact on their health and employment.

Two, a market based on property and ownership would suggest that vendors can designate the recipients of their organs. This is contrary to the ethical principle of allocation based on need.

And three, organ shortage is a global phenomenon and an "ethical market" will presuppose a level playing field among countries and require international harmonisation of regulations.

The nation's reputation as a medical hub can be eroded significantly if it is seen as exploitative, particularly in the current global context where human rights doctrine prohibits exploitative practices. It can be argued that fair compensation, health insurance, and appropriate follow-up care, etc., can be made to potential vendors.

This however would result in significant increased costs for the national healthcare system, resulting in either less transplantation being done or fewer resources dedicated to other health-care needs.

It has been argued that the supply of organs will increase with an organ market, resulting in more lives saved. This is debatable, given that an organ trade may reduce altruistic donation (of both live and cadaveric organs) and will attract predominantly the poor who may provide marginal organs for transplantation.

It has been further argued that people should be allowed to sell their organs so long as the benefit–risk ratio is favourable. One should however look at both the short-term and long-term benefit–risk ratio.

In the short term, vendors may not have access to or be able to afford appropriate care. In the long term, given the increasing incidence of longer life expectancy and end-stage organ failure, the vendors themselves may be in need of transplantation.

The Declaration that was issued from the Istanbul summit emphasised the need for practices that support organ donation from dead donors.

It also called on all countries to address their responsibilities with respect to exploitative practices and to develop self-sufficiency in organ donation.

The current organ shortage requires the international community to cooperate in finding solutions and ending unethical practices.

3

Government Reward for Kidney Donations Is Necessary

Sally Satel

Sally Satel is resident scholar at the American Enterprise Institute, and she is the editor of When Altruism Isn't Enough: The Case for Compensating Kidney Donors.

The number of available kidneys for transplant is chronically low in relation to the number of donors who need them. Although many solutions to this problem have been presented, government rewards seem to offer the best possible answer. After all, people who sign up for the U.S. military are compensated for their contribution to the safety of the nation. Therefore, a government-administered award to organ donors seems to be an appropriate way of thanking those people who risk their lives for the benefit of others.

In early 2006, Matt Thompson of San Jose, California, decided to give a kidney to Sonny Davis, a 65-year-old physicist living in nearby Menlo Park. Thompson was moved to donate after reading an impassioned plea from Davis's wife, who had sent 140 letters to friends and relatives asking them to consider helping her husband. One of the recipients happened to be a colleague of Thompson's, who passed it along, thinking Thompson just might heed the call. Sure enough, Thompson, a devout young Christian and former missionary, contacted the transplant program to volunteer.

Sally Satel, "When Altruism Isn't Moral," *The American: The Journal of the American Enterprise Institute*, January 30, 2009. Copyright © 2009 American Enterprise Institute for Public Policy Research. Reproduced with the permission of the American Enterprise Institute for Public Policy Research, Washington, D.C.

But the transplant program at Kaiser Permanente of Northern California turned him down. Had Davis been a family member or a good friend, he would have been acceptable to the program. Thompson was frustrated and surprised, but he and Davis were determined to do the transplant. According to the *San Jose Mercury News*, they "knew they had to forge a bond that would assure Davis' surgeons that Thompson was donating his kidney for the right reasons." This meant, among other things, that Thompson would not profit financially. So the two developed a relationship and convinced the transplant program that no money was secretly being exchanged. On November 14, 2006, the transplant finally took place.

Far more than a human interest tale of a stranger opening his heart to a suffering soul, the story of Sonny Davis and Matt Thompson draws back the curtain on the culture of the organ transplant establishment. It shows that transplant professionals would have allowed a 65-year-old man to languish on dialysis for years or die—a strong probability given his age—while waiting for a kidney, out of fear that he might be remunerating someone for an act that would save his life.

A non-cash reward won't appeal to those in desperate need of financial help. What they want is quick cash, not delayed in-kind rewards.

There are about 78,000 people in queue for a kidney from a deceased donor. In places like California, the wait can be up to eight years. And unless a friend or relative gives a kidney to a loved one, he will weaken on dialysis. Four thousand people die each year because they cannot survive the wait. This explains Mrs. Davis's frantic plea to anyone who might volunteer a kidney to her husband.

Altruism Is Not Enough

The woeful inadequacy of our nation's transplant policy is due to its reliance on "altruism." According to the guiding narrative of the transplant establishment, organs should be a "gift of life," an act of selfless generosity. It's a beautiful sentiment, no question. In fact, I, myself, am a poster girl for altruism. In 2006, I received a kidney from a (formerly) casual friend who heard secondhand about my need for a transplant. In her act, there was everything for me to gain, and, frankly, not much for her. My glorious donor was moved by empathy and altruism as purely as anyone could ever be.

Yet, it is lethally obvious that altruism is not a valid basis for transplant policy. If we keep thinking of organs solely as gifts, there will never be enough of them. We need to encourage more living and posthumous donation through rewards, say, tax credits or lifetime health insurance.

But what about the Matt Thompson–Sonny Davis problem: anxiety surrounding the very notion that an organ donor should receive anything of material value for his sacrifice. It is important to understand the nature of this anxiety because it is a formidable obstacle to devising a rational transplant system.

Yet, our current altruism-only system has a dark side. It imposes coercion of its own by putting friends and family members in a bind.

Some Oppose Incentives

Arguments against creating incentives to donate fall into two general categories: arguments from corruption and arguments from consequence. These designations were coined by political philosopher Michael Sandel.

Arguments from consequence go like this: there is nothing intrinsically wrong with compensating donors, but it is not possible to design an incentive-based system without exploiting them. The worry is that economic straits could compel reluctant individuals to relinquish a kidney for the sole sake of enrichment.

This is indeed a troubling situation. Fortunately, it can be addressed with good policy. For example, a state government could provide compensation such as tax credits, tuition vouchers, a contribution to a tax-free retirement account, or lifelong health coverage. A non-cash reward won't appeal to those in desperate need of financial help. What they want is quick cash, not delayed in-kind rewards. A months-long waiting period would dampen impulsivity and give more than ample time for donor education and careful medical and psychological screening. Finally, donors would receive quality follow-up care, something the current system does not ensure.

Arguments from corruption proceed from the belief that donors, and perhaps society at large, will be diminished or corrupted if organs are given in return for something of material value. Giving a kidney "for free" is noble but accepting compensation is illegitimate, a sordid affront to human dignity. Indeed, the debate surrounding incentives for organ donation sometimes resembles a titanic struggle between uplift and greed. "As a rule, the debate is cast as one in which existing relations of selfless, altruistic exchange are threatened with replacement by market-based, for-profit alternatives," observes Kieran Healy, a sociologist at Duke University.

Dr. Luc Noel of the World Health Organization subscribes to this false choice. "There are two prevailing concepts of transplantation," he says. "One relies on money and leads to increased inequality, besides putting a price on the integrity of the body and human dignity. The second is based on solidarity and the donor's sole motivation to save a life." The National Kidney Foundation warns against "self-interest on behalf of the donor." The notion also troubles a primary care physician in Columbus, Ohio: "What sort of organ transplant program do we want," he asks, "one that pressures the financially vulnerable with cash incentives, or one that encourages the show of kindness through a loving, voluntary gift of organ donation?"

Our Current System Is Flawed

Paradoxically, our current transplant system makes every donation seem like a "loving, voluntary gift of organ donation." Think about it: there is no other legal option. Some altruistic donations come as close to the technical definition: my experience would be one of those. Yet, our current altruism-only system has a dark side: It imposes coercion of its own by putting friends and family members in a bind. They might not want to donate, but they feel obligated, lest their relative die or deteriorate on dialysis. Sociologists have written about familial dynamics that involve guilt, overt pressure, or subtle threats. Consider the "black-sheep donor," a wayward relative who shows up to offer an organ as an act of redemption, hoping to reposition himself in the family's good graces. Some donate as a way to elicit praise and social acceptance. For others, donation is a sullen fulfillment of familial duty, a way to avoid the shame and guilt of allowing a relative to suffer needlessly and perhaps even die.

Financial and humanitarian motives do not reside in discrete realms.

As famed anthropologist Marcel Mauss observed in his classic work, *The Gift*, gifts are never free; they demand reciprocity. "The [given] objects are never completely separated from the men who exchange them," he learned from his work with Polynesian natives in the early 1900s. The same applies to organs. The "tyranny of the gift" is an artful term coined by sociologists Renee Fox and Judith Swazey to capture the way in which immense gratitude at receiving a kidney can morph into a sense of constricting obligation. In their 1992 book, *Spare Parts: Organ Replacement in American Society*, the authors write, "The giver, the receiver, and their families, may find themselves locked in a creditor-debtor vise that binds them one to another in a mutually fettering way." Indeed, the virtue of market-like exchanges is that they are emotionally liberating.

Altruism Would Not Vanish

An unusual take on altruism comes from the National Kidney Foundation [NKF], a vocal opponent of incentivizing organ donation. According to Dolph Chianchiano, its senior vice president for health policy and research, the NKF believes that compensating donors will "cheapen the gift." Such an affront to would-be donors will cause them to hold onto their organs. On one level, this seems absurd. Can you imagine a brother telling his ailing sister, "Gee, sis, I would have given you my kidney but now that I hear that someone across town is accepting a tax credit for his donation, well, forget it."

It is all too easy to romanticize altruism.

But if Chianchiano is correct—that some people will withhold voluntary action if remuneration is available to others—then, paradoxically, a regime of donor compensation would be quite the boon to such "altruists." They would have bragging rights: They were the ones who acted out of generosity, not for material gain, a distinction that not only allows them to retain the "warm glow" that comes from performing acts of charity but also intensifies it. Given the importance of "social signaling" through gift-giving ("look at me, so generous, so civic-minded!") the opportunity to accentuate the distinction should be most welcome.

No wonder scholars ranging from philosophers to evolutionary biologists to psychologists and economists are skeptical about whether true human altruism even exists. It is more realistic to envision a broad middle ground between the poles of selflessness and greed. It is the arena in which most organ donation already plays out. And it is where compensated donation would likely reside, too.

Simply look at our daily lives. Financial and humanitarian motives do not reside in discrete realms. Moreover, it is unclear how their comingling is inherently harmful—the goodness of an act is not diminished because someone was paid to perform it. The great teachers who enlighten us and the doctors who heal us inspire no less gratitude because they are paid. A salaried firefighter who risks her life to save a child trapped in a burning building is no less heroic than a volunteer firefighter. Soldiers accept military pay while pursuing a patriotic desire to serve their country. The desire to do well by others while enriching oneself at the same time is as old as humankind. Indeed, the very fact that generosity and remuneration so often intertwine can be leveraged to good ends: to increase the pool of transplantable organs, for instance.

The Body's Value In History

The practice of assigning values to body parts has roots in antiquity. The Code of Hammurabi provides an elaborate schedule of compensation for them; for example, it specifics that if an individual should "knock out the teeth of a freed man, he shall pay one-third of a gold *mina*." Today we routinely assign valuation to the body. Human blood plasma is collected primarily though paid donation. Personal injury lawyers seek damages for bodily harm to their clients. The Veterans Administration puts a price on physical disabilities. We pay for justice in the context of personal injury litigation in the form of legal costs, and for our very lives in the form of medical fees. There is little reason to believe—nor tangible evidence to suggest—that these practices depreciate human worth or undermine human dignity in any way.

It is all too easy to romanticize altruism. Sociologist Amitai Etzioni urges the postponement of paying for organs in favor of what he calls a "communitarian" approach "so that members of society will recognize that donating one's organs . . . is the moral (right) thing to do . . . it entails a moral dialogue, in which the public is engaged, leading to a change in what people expect from one another." Thomas A. Shannon, a professor of religion and social ethics, writes, "I would think it a tragedy if . . . we tried to solve the problem of the organ shortage by commodification rather than by the kindness of strangers who meet in the community and recognize and meet the needs of others in generosity."

To be sure, these skeptics have a right to their moral commitments, but their views must not determine binding policy in a morally pluralistic society. A donor compensation system operating in parallel with our established mechanism of altruistic procurement is the only way to accommodate us all. Moreover, it represents a promising middle ground between the status quo—a procurement system based on the partial myth of selfless altruism—and the dark, corrupt netherworld of organ trafficking. The current regime permits no room for individuals who would welcome an opportunity to be rewarded for rescuing their fellow human beings; and for those who wait for organs in vain, the only dignity left is that with which they must face death.

4

Government Interference Would Hamper Kidney Donations

Dan McDougall

Dan McDougall is a foreign correspondent who specializes in south Asian issues for the Observer.

Despite efforts to eliminate the sale of organs throughout the world, an underground organ market exists in many countries. The tsunami that ravaged southeast Asia in 2004 increased the poverty in the region, and some of the poorest residents have resorted to selling their organs to rich Asians and Westerners to help provide for their families. Unfortunately, many of these donors are not paid what they have been promised and go on to suffer severe physical and emotional pain from their loss. On the other hand, if the government regulated the organ market, fewer organs would be available to the dying patients who need them.

The pain is hardest to take at night, says V Kala, as she lifts the crumpled folds of her faded cotton sari to expose a 13-inch scar across her midriff. 'I lie awake in agony scratching and clutching at the side of my body. Sometimes it feels like it is still there, throbbing inside of me. It's at this time I feel most alone with what I've done. The doctors told me to expect that. I don't want sympathy or kind words. I want you to understand why I have put myself through this. It was my decision to sell my kidney. My family was drowning in debt.'

Poverty as Motivation

Just over a month ago, Kala, 32, a mother of three, had stood shaking with fear in Chennai's [India] decrepit Kaliappa hospital. With her were an organ broker, a local advocate clutching her sworn affidavit saying that the recipient was a relative, a doctor and the elderly patient her kidney was destined for.

'The broker told me not to bring anyone close to me, in case they changed my mind. The only person in the room I could relate to was the dying woman lying on the bed. What struck me as surprising was her age,' said Kala. 'She was 80, from a Brahmin caste. She looked rich, like she'd had a good life. She told me she wanted to live longer to see her grandchildren in America. I wanted to help; now I feel betrayed. I've inherited her suffering.'

The cash-for-kidneys business continues, mainly in small private hospitals where regulations are weak and technology plentiful.

Kala walks painfully back towards her dismal concrete hut in Ernavoor, a desolate fishing village an hour's drive north of Chennai. Trapped on a sliver of mud between the ocean and the Adyar river, it is one of many poor hamlets strung along the Bay of Bengal ravaged by the 2004 tsunami. Behind the long rows of single dwellings, built by the government to compensate fishermen who lost their homes, hunchback cows graze in vast, rotting piles of rubbish. The filthy sea estuary in the distance emits the sulphurous smells of poverty and sewage.

Here in this ravaged community of 2,500 people, the *Observer* found 51 women who have sold kidneys in the past six months to escape the pressures of loan sharks who preyed on them after the tsunami. The majority of donors are women in their twenties. The recipients are both Western and Indian, and rich.

'At least 80 people we know of have given their organs in recent months, most are women, but the figure may be 10 times as much,' says S Maria Silva, head of Ernavoor's tsunami fishermen's association. 'Our community is little more than a refugee camp, made up of eight tsunami-affected villages. After the tsunami we were moved to a temporary village known as Kargil Nagar, but it went up in flames and we were forced here, 14km [about nine miles] from our fishing boats. The fishermen here are literally washed up; they can't afford the commute to their boats. Their wives put food on the table now. They either sell firewood and coconut husks from dawn to dusk and still starve, or they sell their organs to keep heads above water.'

An Underground Organ Market Remains

Before passing a series of laws attempting to ban the practice, India was the worst offender in the global organ trade. In cities such as Mumbai, foreigners could easily obtain transplants, although the level of medical care and likely success of the operation varied. The Indian government insists those days are gone, but the cash-for-kidneys business continues, mainly in small private hospitals where regulations are weak and technology plentiful. A hospital needs only a blood supply, dialysis machine and post-operative care facilities to carry out a transplant.

As people live longer, increasing the demand for organs, supplies diminish, thanks to increased survival rates in intensive care units.

According to Dr. Ravindranath Seppan, of the Chennai Doctors' Association for Social Equality, which campaigns against the trade, the situation is desperate. He said: 'Although India banned commercial trading in human organs in 1994, it is clear a lucrative underground market has emerged in

Chennai's suburbs. India's rich are turning to India's poor to live longer, and as the economy grows this abominable situation will also grow.'

Dr. Seppan points to a study published in the *Journal of the American Medical Association* where researchers surveyed 305 Indians who had sold their kidneys, and found 96 per cent had done so to pay off debts, but three-quarters remained in debt and 86 per cent said their health had seriously declined since the operation. The World Health Organisation issued guidelines in 1991 to avoid the exploitation of organ donors. They were endorsed by 192 countries, including the UK, but are not binding. And at least one country, Iran, has a legally regulated system to trade organs.

As health care increasingly becomes a marketplace transaction, a fierce debate about commercialising transplants has emerged. On one side are campaigners such as Dr. Seppan, who believe the poor suffer, and on the other side, many who believe that payments can only help the dire shortage of organs for those who desperately need them.

One of Britain's top kidney consultants, Dr. Andy Stein, of Walsgrave Hospital, Coventry, called last week for the organ trade to be legalised, claiming that donors will suffer if it continues to go underground. As people live longer, increasing the demand for organs, supplies diminish, thanks to increased survival rates in intensive care units. Improved road safety has also cut the number of organs obtained from car crash victims. Frustrated by NHS [National Health Service] waiting lists, unknown numbers of sick Britons go abroad to find brokers, some of whom offer kidneys illicitly harvested from slums in countries such as China, India, the Philippines and those in eastern Europe.

But the internet offers the easiest solution. In 2004, bids for a human kidney reached $5.7m on eBay, before the company shut the sale down. An eBay spokesman later admitted: 'From time to time, we get a kidney or a liver.' The company classes such sales in the same category as people who try to sell rocket launchers, and close down the site after informing the police.

The Pain Continues

Maria Silva and other women from Ernavoor, who complain of excruciating pain in the wake of operations, are now taking matters into their own hands. A fortnight ago, dozens of residents marched on the house of Prakesh Babu, a local broker responsible for 15 sales in the past four months, demanding his arrest.

V Mary, who sold her kidney through Babu, said: 'We don't expect him to resurface. He fled when we went to his home. Babu persuaded me to sell. I was paid 35,000 rupees (£460) and he told me he cut himself 8,000 rupees (£100), but I know he took 10 times as much.'

Mary's hut is a cramped room with a dirt floor, shared by a family of five. It is suffocating in the heat. She admits her estranged husband frittered away most of what was left on drink after the moneylender was paid.

Mary's neighbour, S Rani, 36, is clearly in pain. She sold her kidney to pay her 23-year-old daughter's debt to a local hospital. 'My daughter had a caesarean when she had my grandson and lost a lot of blood. She spent a month in hospital, running up a bill of 30,000 rupees. To make matters worse, my son-in-law's family was demanding a 20,000-rupee (£290) dowry debt and my husband had run away. I went to the hospital gates looking for a broker and I had the operation a month later in another hospital in Chennai. I woke up twice during the operation and was sent home after only two days with a handful of sedatives.'

She said: 'My broker was Shana Lakshmi. She once sold her own kidney and now she helps sell others. I was promised 1.5 lakh (£2,000) but only got 40,000. She paid me on the train platform on the way home, and I was in too much pain.

I had to take what I was given. Now I can hardly walk.' Rani's daughter runs towards us waving her mother's medical files—written in English, which she can't read, asking me to translate.

This system may seem horrendous to you, but it may not seem quite so bad when your family is starving in a gutter.

In the fluorescent light of the dialysis ward of the Kaliappa hospital, feeble patients sit in armchairs hooked up to ancient fridge-sized machines that simulate the job of the kidney: it's a life-preserving process for people whose kidneys have failed, but they have to be connected three hours at a time, three days a week.

Outside the ward, Rana Vishnawatan, an elderly Indian businessman, drinks from a water fountain: 'My kidney is failing and I don't want to be one of those people in there getting my blood changed in and out of the machine like a car going for an oil change,' he says. 'Nor can I afford dialysis. You tell me, what choice do I have? My family is looking for a broker. Either one comes to me or I make one come. I don't have much time.'

'This system may seem horrendous to you, but it may not seem quite so bad when your family is starving in a gutter. The kidney business is not a trade—understand that—but a form of co-operation. It is not buying or selling. One person is dying of hunger. The other has money, but is on dialysis three or four times a week. If we all decide to cooperate, we can help save each other.'

Organ Donations Are for the Good of Humanity

The Church of England

The Church of England, which celebrates the Christian faith, is the largest church in Great Britain.

The Christian faith is rooted in caring and compassion for others. Voluntary organ donation is in line with that faith. Therefore, Christians are encouraged to donate their organs for the good of humanity as long as they are not coerced. In addition, donors should not receive any material gain for their organs. Above all else, the human body should be respected along with the wishes of surviving family members.

Giving oneself and one's possessions voluntarily for the well-being of others and without compulsion is a Christian duty of which organ donation is a striking example, the Church of England has told the House of Lords. The Church's Mission and Public Affairs Division was responding to the Lords' EU [European Union] Social Policy and Consumer Affairs sub-committee's inquiry into the EU Commission's Communication on organ donation and transplantation: policy actions at EU level.

"Christians have a mandate to heal, motivated by compassion, mercy, knowledge and ability," the response says. "The Christian tradition both affirms the God-given value of human bodily life, and the principle of putting the needs of others before one's own needs."

The Church of England, "Organ Donation a Christian Duty," Church of England, October 8, 2007. www.cofe.anglican.org. Reproduced by permission.

The response repeats the Church's opposition to selling organs for commercial gain, while accepting organs being freely given by living donors, with no commercial gain. It argues that, if the present opt-in system of organ donation is to continue, it will need to be backed by a properly resourced programme of public awareness-building and education.

Christian faith is a positive motivation for organ donation and a powerful incentive for many people to donate.

Whether organ donation should be arranged through an "opt-in" or an "opt-out" system is not a question on which Christians hold a single set of views, the response explains. The opt-in system, where people sign up to be donors if they die, reflects Christian concern 'to celebrate and support gracious gifts, freely given'. An opt-out approach, where people state that they do not wish to donate organs, 'could stress the Christian concern for human solidarity and living sacrificially for others'.

The response goes on to say: "The undoubted need for more organs to be donated for the healing of others has to be weighed against the changed relationship between persons and the State which moving to an opt-out system could entail." Either way, all EU member states would need to adopt the same opt-out or opt-in approach to consent for organ donation, it argues.

Christianity Supports Organ Donation

1. The terms of reference of the Church of England's Mission and Public Affairs Unit require it to assist the Church in making a constructive and informed response to issues facing contemporary society. The Unit reports to the Archbishops' Council and, through it, to the General Synod, the Parliament of the Church of England.

2. The Mission and Public Affairs Division warmly welcomes the opportunity to respond to the House of Lords' Committee's call for evidence on organ donation and transplantation. In particular we would like our responses to be seen as addressing your request to consider questions that may arise from a faith-based point of view, even though they also largely address the issues raised in the first part of your call for evidence. We would like to emphasise that Christian faith is a positive motivation for organ donation and a powerful incentive for many people to donate.

3. For Christians, acts of mercy are a part of the self-sacrifice that God requires of us. Christ is the paradigm of self-giving. Giving oneself and one's possessions voluntarily for the well being of others and without compulsion is a Christian duty.

4. Christians have a mandate to heal, motivated by compassion, mercy, knowledge and ability.

Selling organs for commercial gain would never follow from a Christian ethic.

---

5. The Christian tradition both affirms the God-given value of human bodily life, and the principle of putting the needs of others before one's own needs. Organ donation is a striking example of this.

6. Whether organ donation should be arranged through an 'opt-in' or an 'opt-out' system is not a question on which Christians hold a single set of views. The opt-in system reflects our concern to celebrate and support gracious gifts, freely given. The opt-out approach stresses Christian concern for human solidarity and living sacrificially for others. We are also concerned to understand moral questions like this in their wider social and political context and, here, the undoubted need for more organs to be donated for the healing

of others has to be weighed against the changed relationship between persons and the State which moving to an opt-out system might entail.

Respecting Donors

7. Selling organs for commercial gain would never follow from a Christian ethic. It confuses the notion of an organ as gift and turns it into a commodity.

8. However, altruistic organ donation from a living donor would flow from a Christian ethic, provided there was no co-ercion, no commercial gain, and above all no harm to the living donor. That the organ might go anonymously to a recipient, unknown and unrelated to the donor, only heightens the self-giving of the donor.

9. If the present opt-in system is to continue, it will need to be backed by a properly resourced programme of public awareness-building and education.

10. Our experience as pastors . . . has shown us that the body is crucially important to bereaved parents and friends. There were numerous requests for burial services for body parts of children that had already been buried. The body is to be respected and the continuity between life and death in the form of what is done with the body matters. The body at its burial or cremation should ideally be recognizably the body of the person who has died.

11. However, though body parts must always be treated reverently, they should not be mistaken for the person him- or herself. The reverence is perhaps expressed best in the use of body parts only and always for healing others. The harvesting of organs should not be such as to violate this continuity or to cause unnecessary distress to the mourners.

12. It is extremely important to be clear about the point of death, particularly when there is a pressure to maintain organs in a healthy state before harvesting them. This, again, is of vital importance to the bereaved.

13. We welcome the potential for Europe-wide organization of organ transplant services if a just system can be devised: member states will need to ensure that there is a balance between the organs they can provide and those their citizens need for transplant otherwise some nations will be jeopardized and worse off than hitherto. For example, all member states would need to adopt the same opt-out or opt-in approach to consent for organ donation.

6

The Use of Human Organs Undermines Humanity

Gilbert Meilaender

Gilbert Meilaender is the Richard and Phyllis Duesenberg Professor of Christian Ethics at Valparaiso University and a former member of the President's Council on Bioethics.

Recently, Gordon Brown, prime minister of Great Britain, proposed that healthy organs be harvested for transplantation from the recently deceased unless they signed an opt-out form. Although the demand for organs has greatly surpassed the supply, Brown's proposal treats the human body as community property. In an age where human organs are being bought and sold on the black market, any attempt to acquire organs without the expressed consent of donors is a dangerous proposition. In fact, the ethical implications of organ transplantation in general have yet to be resolved.

In *The Patient as Person*, published almost forty years ago, when transplantation technology was still in its early stages, Paul Ramsey considered different ways of procuring organs for transplant. One might invite people to "opt in," to donate organs to be used after their death (or, in the case of a paired organ such as the kidney, even before death). One might require people to "opt out" if they did not wish to have their organs taken after death for transplant, presuming consent unless they (while living) or their next of kin (after their death) specifically declined to consent. Or one might establish some kind of system whereby organs needed for transplant could be bought and sold (though he was thinking only of cadaver organs).

The third of these possibilities should, Ramsey believed, be rejected altogether. But his verdict with respect to the first two was more nuanced, a comparison of their relative merits and demerits. "If giving is better than routinely taking organs to prolong the lives of patients needing transplants, then it must also be said that routinely taking them in hospital practice would be better than for us to make medical progress and extend treatment to patients by means of buying and selling cadaver organs. That society is a better and more civilized one, I have said, in which men join together in a consensual community to effect these purposes, than a society in which lives are saved routinely, without the positive consent and will of all concerned to do so. It must also be said, however, that a society would be better and more civilized in which men are joined together routinely in making cadaver organs available to prolong the lives of others than one in which this is done ostensibly by consent to the 'gift' but actually for the monetary gain of the 'donor.'"

An increasing number of voices supports some form of payment for organs.

Responding to Brown's Proposal

I recalled this passage when reading of the recent proposal by Gordon Brown, prime minister of Great Britain, to deal with what he called "an avoidable human tragedy" by encouraging more people to "donate" organs. Britain's National Health Service, Brown suggested on January 14, 2008, should move to a system in which organs of the deceased would be taken for transplant, with their consent presumed, unless before death they had opted out or, after death, their family members objected to such use of their organs.

Ramsey's comparative analysis might remind us that the prime minister's proposal is not the worst we can envision. Ours is a world in which an increasing number of voices support some form of payment for organs (or, sometimes, for organs from specific populations, such as prisoners nearing death)—thereby turning potential donors into vendors and the body into a collection of parts that are available and alienable if the price is right. This would, Ramsey seemed to think, and I am inclined to agree, be worse than what Mr. Brown has in mind.

Nor, I think, will it do to object to Mr. Brown's proposal on the ground that my body is my property alone, no part of which should be taken or used without my explicit consent. There are, after all, occasions—if, for example, an autopsy is deemed necessary—when we allow the needs of the larger society to override the bodily integrity of a deceased individual. More important, though, is that "property" does not seem to be the right way to think of my body's relation to me. Thinking in those terms may, in fact, leave us defenseless in the face of arguments supporting a market in organs.

A person does not belong, to the whole extent of his being, to any earthly community.

Nor is the body of the deceased best thought of as property of his surviving family. If their wishes about its disposal ought to be honored, that is not because they own the body. It is because the life they shared with this one who has died obligates them to give his body proper burial—and the rest of us should do nothing that makes their duty more onerous than it of necessity is or that forces them, while grieving, to fight for the right to carry out such a fundamental human duty. "There is," as [Southern Methodist Univeristy emeritus professor of ethics] William F. May once put it, "a tinge of the inhuman in the humanitarianism of those who believe that the perception of social need easily overrides all other considerations."

Examining Brown's Language

Still, there are good reasons to draw back from procuring organs for transplant by means of an opt-out system. We need an [author George] Orwell among us to note how strained the language of those, like Mr. Brown, becomes when they describe what they have in mind. His aim, he wrote, is "a different consent system" that would "increase donation levels" significantly. But, of course, it is not really "donation" that he has in mind. It is taking, not giving—and a consent that must be presumed is one that only the articulate and the powerful are likely to avoid giving. Those from whom the organs are taken, whose consent is presumed, might better be thought of as useful resources than as donors. Moreover, it would place a special burden on some groups whose beliefs—often, religious beliefs—lead them (except in special circumstances) to object to the giving or taking of bodily organs after death.

The prime minister's language—of "an avoidable human tragedy" that could be averted were more organs available for transplant—is the sort of talk that has come to characterize most discussions of transplantation, and it begs for careful examination. It is the sort of language that can be used to justify almost anything that promises to help avoid the tragedy of death. And this is exactly the sort of language that, we have come to see, has often distorted the practice of medicine, teaching us to suppose that anything that can be done to ward off death must be done. But the deeper moral truth is that how we live, not how long, is what matters most. And among the possible "tragedies" with which we must reckon would be to live longer by means that debase or undermine our humanity.

The Human Body Is Not Property

Why is giving of organs better than taking, even if taking may provide a greater supply for transplant? To look on potential "donors" chiefly as handy collections of spare parts to be used by others is to lose the sense of the embodied human person as one who, because made finally for God, transcends every location in space and time. A person does not belong, to the whole extent of his being, to any earthly community.

Even the deceased person does not. Why, for example, did an al-Qaeda-led group in Iraq release footage of two corpses that it said were those of U.S. soldiers killed in June 2006? The video showed a decapitated body and several dead bodies being stepped on. This dishonoring of the corpses could have no point were not even the dead body still a reminder of the presence of the person, who can be the "property" of none of us, not merely a "resource" to be used for our purposes, however important they may be.

To see this, however, is to begin to see the deepest truth of all: Even the giving of organs for transplant is not unproblematic. If we first see how troubling even the giving is, we can understand why, if organs are used, they should be given rather than taken.

Human beings are animals, but not just animals. They are almost godlike in some of their powers, but are not gods. To honor and uphold the dignity of our humanity requires that we respect the peculiar nature of this in-between condition. A person is present to us and among us only as one who is embodied—even if also somehow more than body. And we, in turn, know ourselves not simply as a collection of organs but as a unified living being: not reason or will alone, not physical strength or spirit alone, but an integrated union of body, mind, will, and spirit.

Thus, as neurologist-psychologist Erwin Straus once wrote, the truth that "only with eyes can we see" does not mean that we see with the eyes. On the contrary, it is the person, that unified living being, who sees. "Seeing is," as Straus put it, "located neither in the eye, nor in the retina, nor in the optic nerve ... the brain does not see." It is the person who sees. For certain limited purposes, we may think of or reduce the embodied person to a collection of parts, thinking of the person (from below, as it were) simply as the sum total of those parts. But we do not know either ourselves or others that way.

[Taking organs] does go a long way toward treating persons as handy repositories of interchangeable parts.

Organ Transplantation Changes Our Views of Humanity

All organ transplantation, therefore, even when organs are given, not taken or purchased, invites us to think of ourselves and others in ways that risk the loss of the full meaning of our embodied humanity. All organ transplantation—even when undertaken for the best of reasons and even when justified—remains troubling. It tempts us to think of the body, in terms Paul Ramsey used, as just an "ensemble of parts," just a resource.

But a gift cannot so easily be severed from its giver. When an organ is freely given, that gift—like all gifts—carries with it the presence of the giver and directs our attention back to one who is not just a collection of alienable parts but a unified living being. Indeed, what the donor gives is not simply an organ but himself or herself. The gift can never be entirely severed or alienated from the giver. (Which is why, for example, we would think it wrong for a living donor to give an unpaired vital organ, such as the heart. The gift would undermine the very integrity of bodily life that it aimed to express.)

Taking organs, however, even under the somewhat euphemistic [a mild or vague term to describe something actually harsh] rubric of presumed consent, is a quite different matter.

Although it does not alienate the organ from the person as decisively as would a system of buying and selling organs, it does go a long way toward treating persons as handy repositories of interchangeable parts. Learning to think of ourselves and others that way would be the true human tragedy and may still, just barely, be "an avoidable human tragedy"—to adapt Prime Minister Brown's words to my own quite different purpose.

We will avoid it, though, only to the degree that we cease to be simply cheerleaders in the cause of transplantation and regain, instead, an older wisdom of and about the meaning of the body. Fortified in that way, and aware of what is troubling about all organ transplantation, we will be better able to think about how it may be done right and how it should not be done even in the name of avoiding tragedy.

7

The Selling of Body Parts
Can Benefit the Poor

Bart Croughs

*Bart Croughs is a writer from Holland who focuses on interna-
tional social issues.*

*The world's poor should not be prohibited from selling their or-
gans. Doing so results in the deaths of patients in need of transplants and continued poverty for people who are willing to give.
Although opponents of a legal organ trade argue that buying organs from the poor is simply exploitation, exchanging organs for
money is not much different than working for a paycheck. Ultimately, the decision to sell body parts should be left up to each
individual. Legalizing the organ trade can not only save the lives
of dying patients, it can also improve the standard of living of
thousands of others.*

The problem of organ shortage for transplants is well-
known. In the United States alone, over 80,000 people are
on the waiting list for an organ transplant. Every year, thousands of patients die while waiting for their transplant. What
is the cause of this persistent shortage?

How many TV sets would reach the market if television
manufacturers were not allowed to ask for money for their
product? One does not need to be an economist to understand what the consequences of such a policy would be. Yet
this is exactly the policy that exists today with regard to organs: it is illegal to pay or receive money for organs.

Bart Croughs, "A Man's Body, a Man's Right," *Liberty*, vol. 19, June 2005. Reproduced by
permission.

Adam Smith wrote these famous words: "It is not from the benevolence of the butcher, the brewer, or the baker that we expect our dinner, but from their regard to their self-love." The politicians who have prohibited organ trade and the opinion leaders who support this prohibition still fail to grasp this point.

Supply and Demand Should Prevail

This is not rocket science; the harmful consequences of the introduction of a maximum price for goods and services is part of Economics 101. The price mechanism sees to it that supply and demand are in equilibrium. When there is a shortage of a certain product, the price will go up; the higher price makes it more profitable to make the product, which will increase the supply of the product. If the government prohibits the rise of the price of a certain product, thus artificially keeping the price below the market price, the incentive to increase production disappears, and a permanent shortage of the product ensues. For organs a de facto maximum price of $0 has been introduced, with predictable results.

Politicians often come up with new interventions, with no results to speak of. The only thing politicians do not consider abolishing is the initial intervention which has caused all the misery.

Organ trade is illegal in most countries. India was a well-known exception, where organs were openly traded on a large scale, until the practice was prohibited in the mid-'90s. Organ trade in India was limited primarily to live donors selling a kidney. In the early '90s, a donor received a sum of money for his kidney equaling six times the average annual income in India. The extra supply of kidneys was not only used for kidney patients in India; patients from all over the world who had been put on waiting lists in their home country flooded in.

Why the Prohibition of Organ Trade?

Most who oppose organ trade recognize that paying for organs will lead to more donor organs becoming available, but object nonetheless, mainly out of ethical considerations.

One of the reasons to prohibit organ trade is, as bioethicist and CNN's private philosopher Jeffrey Kahn puts it, that organ trade "could exploit people who need money and wouldn't donate except for payment."

The reasoning is that people should decide to donate voluntarily; when a poor man proceeds to donate out of a desire to be better off financially, it is no longer a matter of voluntariness but of coercion—the poor man is "forced by poverty." The Bellagio Task Force, a collection of scientists who have taken a stand against organ trade, put it as follows: the poverty and deprivation of organ donors can be "so extreme, that the voluntary character of a sale of an organ remains in doubt."

This argument proves far too much. If the poor should not be allowed to sell a kidney because transactions that are motivated by poverty are a matter of "coercion," then they should not be allowed to take a job at a factory either, or to shine shoes, etc. The poor agree to do any of these only because they are "forced by poverty" to do so. Why should someone be allowed to improve his financial position in one manner but not in another? This question is not answered.

In the most extreme poverty, when the choice is between selling a kidney and starving to death, it is most in the interest of the poor that organ trade is legal.

Of course, there is a substantial difference between factory work and the sale of one's organs: selling an organ entails more risk than working at a factory or shining shoes. In the words of the Bellagio Task Force, the removal of an organ poses a "threat to [the donor's] physical health and bodily integrity." (They also note that "the risk to health in selling one kidney is truly minimal . . . at least in developed countries.") The risk is greater that one will come to regret the donation; because of that, the poor should be protected from themselves, to prevent them from making the wrong decision.

But the argument that the removal of an organ is not without risk also applies to organ donations motivated by altruism—they have exactly the same risks. There is no reason to assume that the risk of regretting an organ donation is greater when you are left with a large sum of money after the transaction, than when you are left with nothing except the satisfaction of having helped someone. (The opposite is more likely: there is a real possibility that the transplanted kidney will be rejected. The person who only donated out of altruism has lost his kidney for nothing; this is not the case for the person who gave up his kidney for financial gain.)

The Poor Do Earn Money

Nonetheless, there is a widespread assumption that the poor person who decides to go through life with one kidney in exchange for a large sum of money makes the wrong decision. For example, in 1998 Atul Gawande, writing for the online magazine *Slate*, argued that the sale of an organ "would be right for so few, if any, that permitting the option makes no sense at all." But on what basis Gawande drew this conclusion remains a mystery. By what magical means can an outsider, who knows nothing of the specific circumstances and preferences of the potential seller, be a better judge of which decision is the right one than the organ seller himself? The probable cause of the popularity of this view is that the relatively prosperous intellectuals and politicians who occupy themselves with these issues would not easily sell a kidney for money themselves, and therefore conclude that people for whom selling a kidney can mean the difference between poverty and relative wealth should not do so either—an understandable error.

In fact, the "forced by poverty" argument can be reversed: the more someone is "forced by poverty" to sell a kidney, the more important it is that organ trade is not prohibited. In the most extreme poverty, when the choice is between selling a kidney and starving to death, it is most in the interest of the poor that organ trade is legal.

The whole idea that actions that are risky should be forbidden is ridiculous anyway. It would mean that working as a taxi driver in New York should be prohibited, just like Formula 1 racing, taming lions, having sex without a condom with homosexual junkies, etc.

Another argument from the "exploitation" category is put forward by anthropologist Nancy Scheper-Hughes, the driving force behind anti-organ-trade organization Organs Watch. She laments the fact that donor organs move "from South to North, from Third to First World, from poor to rich, from black and brown to white and from female to male." That may seem unfair, until you realize that there is also a movement in the other direction: namely, a flow of money from the rich to the poor, from the First World to the Third World, etc. And that flow of money is exactly the reason that the poor are prepared to give up their organs!

The whole idea that inequality in health care on the basis of income is unjust and should therefore be prohibited is sanctimonious nonsense that few people really take seriously.

Moreover, the supply of organs is hardly the only service in which the provider of the service is generally poorer than the one who receives it. According to the reasoning above, the profession of housekeeper, for instance, should be prohibited—what great injustice that the flow of household work goes from the rich to the poor!

Inequality Between the Rich and Poor

Yet another typical objection to organ trade is that inequality between poor and rich could result if people would have to pay for organs. As Jeffrey Kahn phrased it: "it could give rich people the chance to get available organs first."

That possibility cannot be excluded, but at this moment, too, there is inequality: that between the patients who are on the waiting list and die before an organ has become available, and the patients who are lucky enough to make it to the operation. The main thing that legalization of organ sales will do is make more organs available, and therefore fewer people will be part of the unlucky group.

Apparently, those who use this argument do not consider inequality based on luck unjust, but they do consider inequality based on income unjust. But why? When you realize how the current, luck-based system of inequality works, the opposite conclusion makes more sense. Patients who have the money to buy an organ are not allowed to do so; many are therefore prematurely regulated into their graves by the government. How this is just is not evident. At the same time, these unfortunate patients are forced to pay for the operations of those who are lucky enough to survive the waiting list. The fairness of that, too, is questionable at best. People who have the money to buy an organ do not cause other patients not to have that money, and neither are they the cause of those patients' illnesses; it is therefore unclear why it is just to make them financially liable for the cost of other people's organ operations. This is a violation of the elementary legal principle according to which people can...be held [only] liable for the damage they cause.

The whole idea that inequality in health care on the basis of income is unjust and should therefore be prohibited is sanctimonious nonsense that few people really take seriously. Western countries have access to health care that is far better than that of the average inhabitant of the Third World, purely on the basis of higher incomes here. Why should this outrageous inequality continue to exist? Why not lower the level of Western health care to Third World level, and donate the money that is thus saved to the Third World to improve health care over there? The reason why abolishing inequality within a country is so much more popular than abolishing inequality between countries is simple: the desire to collect other people's hard-earned money with impunity is much better developed than the desire to lose your own hard-earned money to others. Considerations of "social justice" and "solidarity" are little more than sorry excuses for the desire to live at the expense of other people.

Financial Gain Is a Legitimate Motive

Another objection against organ trade that is often heard is that giving up organs should be done out of altruism and not out of pursuit of profit. As Jeffrey Kahn puts it: "the risk we run is that society comes to share the view that organ donation is no longer about altruism but about less virtuous motives."

In this view, thinking of one's own interests is so reprehensible that it should be prohibited. This argument is diametrically opposed to the previous argument: this time, the donor should not be prevented from entering into an agreement that would harm him, but he should be prevented from entering into one that would benefit him. It's amusing that both arguments are typically used by the same people.

But even if we assume that the desire to benefit financially from a transaction should be prohibited, the problem remains that far too much is proven with this argument. If giving up organs for financial gain should be prohibited because giving organs away for free is so much more noble and generous, then it is hard to see why, for instance, baking bread for financial gain is acceptable; the logical conclusion of such reasoning is that not only should people give up organs altruistically and non-commercially, but also bake bread, make clothes, build houses, etc. In other words: why only sacrifice the well-being and the life of the people who need organs? If it is so morally superior to sacrifice people on the altar of altruism, why not be consistent and let everyone suffer? Say of the communists what you want, at least they were consistent.

Organs Bought and Stolen

Another argument against organ trade that is often used is that it is reprehensible to "commodify" parts of the human body—i.e., to use them as objects. Nancy Scheper-Hughes denounces the markets: "By their very nature markets are indiscriminate, promiscuous and inclined to reduce everything—including human beings, their labor and even their reproductive capacity—to the status of commodities. . . . [and] nowhere is this more dramatically illustrated than in the booming market in human organs from both living and dead donors."

First of all, it is not markets that tend to reduce organs to the status of objects, but people. The reason for that is simple: both buyer and seller expect to gain and there is no third party involved. So what is the problem? This seems to be a primitive way of thinking: organs are (unconsciously) considered as beings who can think and feel, and should therefore be treated "with respect."

But even if you assume that "commodification" of organs is wrong, it is still unclear why this objection should only apply to organ trade and not to organ donations. Why is an organ that is sold being "treated as an object" and an organ that is given as a present not? Objects such as chairs and tables can both be traded and be given as presents; their status as "object" does not depend on whether anything is exchanged for them. It is hard to see why, when it concerns organs, their status as "objects" should suddenly be dependent on whether money is asked in return. In short, if organ trade should be prohibited because "commodification" of organs is reprehensible, then organ donations should be prohibited as well.

Another practical objection that is often used, as pointed out by the Bellagio Task Force: there are allegations of "babies and children kidnapped and murdered for their organs. Many journalists as well as individuals are convinced that the ready market for organs has stimulated these abuses."

The objections against organ trade do not make sense.

There is not much reason to assume that the risk of organ theft will increase when organ trade is legalized. The present shortage of organs for transplant is the product, at least in part, of the prohibition of organ trade; the supply of organs is low, so the price of an organ is high when a black market develops. When organ trade is legalized, the supply of organs will increase, which will make the price of organs drop. That will make stealing organs less profitable, so criminals will have fewer reasons to do so. And, of course, it's easier for organ traders to defraud organ donors (accepting the organs, but not paying the price that was agreed upon) when organ trade is prohibited. When selling organs is illegal, the victims of fraud are less inclined to go to the police. So rather than an argument against legalizing organ trade, the risk of people being robbed or defrauded of their organs is really an argument in favor of legalizing organ trade.

Even if it were true that the risk of crime would increase if organ trade were legalized, there would still be no reason to prohibit organ trade. People are killed to collect their life insurance; should life insurance therefore be prohibited? People are killed so others can quickly receive their inheritance; should the laws of inheritance therefore be abolished?

The objections against organ trade do not make sense; the result of the prohibition of organ trade is that numerous patients are sentenced to death each year for no good reason, while at the same time numerous poor people are deprived of the chance to improve their standard of living.

Finally, this is also a matter of principle. To whom do my organs belong: me or the state?

A man's body, a man's right!

8

The Selling of Body Parts Exploits the Poor

Albert Huebner

Albert Huebner is a California-based writer who focuses on science issues.

Rich patients in need of organs take advantage of the world's poor. Promises of cash rewards for donations are sometimes not kept and when they are kept, they can be far less than agreed upon. Given these disparities, legal organ trade will always lead to the exploitation of impoverished donors. A better solution to the global shortage of organs might be to adopt a policy of "informed presumed consent" so that when people die their organs can be used unless the deceased had requested otherwise.

In a world where the wealthy set the rules of trade, it was only a matter of time until parts of the human body became a hot cash crop. Not only can the rich afford to buy organs from the desperately poor, they also can use "free market" logic to defend the purchases as ethical. From this perspective, it's a win-win situation in which allegedly equal participants come together. The buyer gets a healthy organ, the seller some needed cash. The roles of the organ brokers and the surgeons are defined as benign, if not downright humane.

The real dynamic is very different. As the trade in organs burgeons, concerned medical anthropologists have set up an

Albert Huebner, "Special Report: Organ Snatchers," *Toward Freedom*, May 2004. Reproduced by permission of the author.

independent research and medical human rights project, Organs Watch, which does fieldwork in many countries around the world. Its investigations reveal that while buyers and sellers may be about equal in their desperation, they are dramatically unequal in all other respects. The buyers are obviously well-off; the sellers, most economically marginal, include the hungry and homeless, debtors, refugees, undocumented workers, and prisoners. The buyers have access to the best modern medical technology; the sellers usually have no access to medical treatment or follow-up care.

The trade in organs has opened up medical and financial connections, creating a new movement of human beings that is part transplant tourism, part traffic in slaves. In one well-traveled route, small groups of Israeli transplant patients take a charter plane to Turkey, where they are matched with kidney sellers from rural Moldova or Romania. The transplants are handled by a pair of surgeons, one Israeli, one Turkish. Another network unites European and North American patients with Philippine kidney sellers in a private Episcopal hospital in Manila, arranged through an independent internet broker who advertises on the web. Meanwhile, a Nigerian doctor/broker facilitates transplants in South Africa or Boston, with a ready supply of poor Nigerian kidney sellers, most of them single women. The purchases are notarized by a distinguished law firm in Lagos.

The donor usually doesn't get much out of the sale, and sometimes there is no payment at all.

As a commodity, the kidney has emerged as the gold standard in this new trade, representing the ultimate collateral against hunger, poverty, and debt. In general, the circulation of kidneys follows the routes of traditional colonialism: from South to North, East to West, poorer to more affluent bodies, black and brown bodies to white ones, female to male, or poor, low-status men to more affluent men. Women are almost never the recipients of purchased organs.

Theft and Complications

Most people are aware that the practice of obtaining organs from cadavers doesn't work very well. The list of patients needing transplants is growing much faster than the number of people who have arranged to give up one or more organs upon death. This imbalance, combined with two relatively recent medical developments, has converted the organs of the Third World poor into a new, if ghoulish, commodity. First, the rate of successful transplants is much higher with organs harvested from living donors. Second, the development of more powerful anti-rejection drugs further improves the success of such transplants.

The donor usually doesn't get much out of the sale, and sometimes there is no payment at all. Nancy Scheper-Hughes, professor of anthropology at UC [University of California] Berkeley and director of Organs Watch, describes the harrowing experience of a young mother and office clerk in São Paolo, Brazil. Laudiceia Da Silva entered a large public hospital there for a routine operation to remove an ovarian cyst. She emerged from the anesthesia in great pain with a 17-inch scar across her side. Her left kidney had been removed.

After giving up an organ under conditions that may be reminiscent of a back-alley abortion, the seller frequently experiences complications . . . usually with no hope of treatment.

When Da Silva tried to sue, hospital officials responded that her "missing kidney" was embedded in the tissue around the cyst. But the explanation was highly improbable. They claimed that the diseased ovary had been "discarded" and furthermore, that crucial medical records had been "misplaced." Yet, the state Medical Ethics Board refused to review the case.

Da Silva and her physician were convinced that her kidney had been stolen for transplant to another, wealthier patient in the hospital. "When rich people look at poor people like us," Da Silva said angrily, "all they can see is a bag of parts."

While outright theft occurs throughout the Third World, the "legitimate" selling of body parts is more widespread and just about as exploitative. The sellers are often tricked or coerced by brokers, they don't always get the promised payment, and even when they are paid, that rarely solves whatever problem prompted them to sell the organ. In fact, the "solution" usually makes matters much worse. After giving up an organ under conditions that may be reminiscent of a back-alley abortion, the seller frequently experiences complications including pain, depression, weakness, and the inability to work, usually with no hope of treatment.

Desperate Choices

Conditions in Moldova, one of the countries monitored by Organs Watch, make it an excellent source of body parts. With the demise of the Soviet Union, the agricultural economy collapsed, compelling much of the population to seek work abroad. Vladimir was typical. A slim young man, his age made him the target of a local kidney hunter named Nina. She baited him with the promise of a good job at a Turkish dry cleaning plant, and arranged for his transport to Istanbul, where he stayed in the basement of a run-down hotel, sharing space with other Moldovan villagers.

Once there, Vladimir learned that he had been recruited for more than pressing pants. Step one was to provide a few pints of blood. As soon as a match was found, he'd be taken to a private hospital to give up his "best" kidney for $3000— less the cost of travel, room and board, and fees for his "handlers." A match was soon found—an elderly man from Israel who came to Istanbul with his own surgeon. The buyer, his surgeon, and hospital officials seemed uninterested in the donor, and how he got there.

When Vladimir protested the plan to remove his kidney, Nina showed up with her pistol-carrying boyfriend. "If I had refused to go along with them," Vladimir said ruefully, "my body, minus both kidneys and who knows what else, could be floating somewhere in the Bosporus Strait." Back in Moldova, he has become both unemployable and unmarriageable in a country where kidney selling is viewed as a form of prostitution.

Selling kidneys doesn't carry the same stigma in the Philippines. Some males lie about their age, and boast about selling a kidney when they are as young as 16. "No one at the hospital asks us for any documents," they told a monitor from Organs Watch. They also admitted to lying about other things, including their medical histories and exposure to tuberculosis, AIDS, dengue, and hepatitis.

Willie, a stevedore [dockworker] in Manila, is older, and his wife fumes at him for not being wiser. But he was desperate, and sold his kidney to a foreigner at a local hospital in the hope of saving two of his children, both very sick. They died anyway, and he used most of the $1200 he was paid for his kidney on their funerals. Like Vladimir, he's no longer able to do hard work because, as he explains, "no one wants a kidney-seller on his work team."

Rationalizing Exploitation

Embracing a supply and demand perspective, transplant specialists and health agencies increasingly view the buying and selling as a satisfying solution to the global scarcity of human organs. They are simply treated as commodities, and the traditional barriers against their trade are being replaced by "regulation." Unfortunately, this doesn't protect the sellers from brutal exploitation.

When Dr. Scheper-Hughes visited the secretary of health for the Philippines, Manuel Dayrit, he was leaning toward two regulatory programs. One allowed the poor to sell a kidney to an organ bank, which would make organs available to any Philippine citizen who needed one. Dayrit was understandably reluctant to discuss just how the government would set a price. The circulation of kidneys goes beyond borders, so any national regulatory program has to compete with a thriving international black market. No matter how benign the regulatory effort, it is doomed to fail under the present barbarous conditions.

One mark of a decent society would be a serious effort to find a compassionate and just solution to the problem.

Dayrit's second program gives a new twist to repealing the death penalty. The government would grant death row prisoners a reprieve, converting their execution to life imprisonment in exchange for the donation of a kidney. In effect, this substitutes mutilation for capital punishment. Supporters of this program take an interesting position: It's not that the death penalty is morally wrong, but rather a terrible waste of human body parts.

This approach does remove money from the equation. But exchanging mutilation for capital punishment isn't much of a victory for human rights. China apparently carries this abuse a step further, reportedly relying almost entirely on capital punishment as a source of organs. Although the official numbers are secret, human rights groups have estimated that China harvests organs from at least 2,000 prisoners a year.

A Humane System Is Needed

In the last few years, steady improvement of transplant technology has made it possible to genuinely improve the quality of a life inhibited or endangered by a failing organ. Due to a shortfall in replacement organs, however, a complete solution may never be possible. One mark of a decent society would be a serious effort to find a compassionate and just solution to the problem. A possible way to reduce, if not completely eliminate, this limitation is "informed presumed consent." This means that all citizens would be considered organ donors at brain death, unless they stipulated their refusal beforehand. This preserves the value of transplantation as a social good, with no one included or excluded on the basis of financial status.

Instead of searching for the best way to assure that the benefits of organ transplantation are shared equitably, however, it's business as usual. Organs needed for the well-being of the rich are harvested from the poor, just as, under traditional colonialism, commodities like sugar, coffee, ivory, and diamonds are harvested in Third World countries and exported to developed nations. The organ trade is the "logical" 21st-century extension of hundreds of years of colonial exploitation. First appropriate labor and its fruits, then the body itself.

9

Organs from Living Family Members Should Be Used as a Last Resort

Nancy Scheper-Hughes

Nancy Scheper-Hughes is the founding director of Organs Watch, an independent, human rights project that investigates organ transplantation around the world.

Using donated organs from living family members is often a poor choice. The patient in need may use kinship bonds to coerce others into donating. In other instances, family members who donate organs may use that gift in order to control the recipient. In recent years, the number of children and grandchildren donating organs to their elders has grown, which might be the result of negative attitudes about using organs from cadavers. Ultimately, organ donation from living, family donors, especially young relatives, should be reconsidered.

In a chilling essay followed by a book-length memoir [*Silent Bond*] of his encounter with Paroxysmal Nocturnal Hemoglobinuria (PNH), a rare blood disease destroying his blood cells, David Biro explained why he felt that any one of his sisters should unhesitatingly offer themselves as blood marrow donors. 'That is what families *are supposed to do*', the young doctor stated, even mildly dysfunctional families like his in which the older brother and his baby sister were, before and

Nancy Scheper-Hughes, "The Tyranny of the Gift: Sacrificial Violence in Living Donor Transplants," *American Journal of Transplantation*, vol. 7, no. 3, March 2007, pp. 507–11. Copyright © 2007 Nancy Scheper-Hughes. Reproduced by permission of Blackwell Publishing Ltd.

after the donor transfer, virtual strangers to each other. Biro describes his younger sister, his future donor: 'My day to day knowledge of Michelle was curiously incomplete . . . We rarely talk about anything deeper than a movie or a meal . . . I loved her in the distracted way you love a person whose external data are familiar but whose internal workings are a pleasant mystery . . . [but] now I needed her.'

Biro felt justified in putting his younger sister's life—the one whose near perfect genetic match turned out to be David's 'jackpot' number—and her mobility on hold indefinitely. A free spirit who had trekked across the Yukon and worked with disabled children in rural Guatemala, Michelle interrupted her life and her travels to serve her brother's medical needs. Although a vegetarian, she agreed to eat plenty of red meat and sing the praises of a slab of Canadian bacon. The possible risks to the donor—excessive pain, delayed or prolonged recovery, anesthesia reactions, injury to tissue, bone or nerves were never mentioned.

In the early decades of transplant physicians were cautious about living donors, realizing that relatives of the sick were often under pressure to donate.

This scenario fits the normative transplant discourse in which gifting and altruism are assumed among close friends and kin. It is what any one of us would hope for ourselves were we in the same predicament, either as donor or recipient. But Michelle's donor role was not over after the transplant. Now that 'she had literally become a part of me', Biro wrote that he wanted to keep her close by him in the event he might suffer a relapse that would require more of her marrow. He admitted to feeling resentment whenever his sister spoke of plans for far-flung journeys and he demanded that she cancel a trip to Alaska. Michelle, the silent and invisible object lesson in this medical parable, quietly acquiesced, or so we assume. Biro saw his medical needs as an automatic future claim over his sister's body, which sustained him physically and psychologically. . . .

At the close of his essay Biro boasts that he never thanked his sister because 'to do so would have violated the pact of silence that brothers and sisters feel compelled to uphold'. This 'pact of silence' is what anthropologists call a 'public secret', something known by all but unstated because of the extreme fragility of the social situation. Here the 'secret' concerns fairly primitive blood claim by one sibling on the other. A living donor in Brazil said that her surgeon had extracted a similar promise that she never speak of her gift within the family as it would be unfair to the recipient. The gift must be invisible, thus maintaining a 'family myth' capable of erupting later on.

Biro's memoir was highly praised as 'the work of a doctor who has the soul of a "poet"'. There is no mention in the reviews of David's donor, illustrating my point that living donors are almost as invisible as deceased ones. Both are faceless 'suppliers' of a scarce commodity. Over time the transplant experience was reduced 'to a wisp of memory' as each moved on in their lives. Biro went back to 'not knowing Michelle and she to not knowing me'. This narrative speaks less to family bonds than to family bondage, less to gifting than to poaching. . . .

In the early decades of transplant physicians were cautious about living donors, realizing that relatives of the sick were often under pressure to donate. Thus, they went out of their way to protect designated donors from having to do so, often providing them with a medical alibi even though this went against their own desires to see their patient transplanted. One surgeon, cited by [researchers R.] Fox and [J.P.] Swazey believed that living donation involved such a degree of interdependence and over-identification between donor and recipient that it ought to be a taboo, similar to the incest taboo. That caution has evaporated as living donor transplant became routine.

The Tyranny of the Gift

In some societies, like Japan, where the demands of gift giving are very elaborate, individuals fear being the recipient of a large and impressive gift that can humiliate the receiver who has no possibility of repaying it. Fox and Swazey first referred to the 'tyranny of the gift' to describe the onus of organs gifting:

> The gift the recipient has received from the donor is so extraordinary that it is inherently unreciprocal. It has no physical or symbolic equivalent. As a consequence, the giver, the receiver, and their families may find themselves locked in a creditor-debtor vise that binds them to each other in a mutually fettering way.

The gift giver may lord it over the recipient and may feel proprietary toward the recipient of their largesse. In my Organs Watch files are examples of the following: a father who gave his 16-year-old son a kidney continues to control his movements well into adulthood, even reading and censoring his love letters; a sister-donor refuses to allow her younger brother to ride his motorcycle or go out to parties where alcohol was served because it might damage 'her' kidney; a donor aunt who rejects the engagement of her niece to a man the aunt deems unworthy of the person *whose life she had saved*. In each case the donor did not give but 'lent' a kidney to the patient.

Thus paying a stranger for a kidney can seem liberating to the buyer. A young Israeli woman who traveled to Durban, South Africa, in 2003 where she was transplanted with a kidney purchased from a poor Brazilian said she had done so to avoid asking a relative to serve as her donor:

> To ask someone from inside your own family, it's too difficult. It's like you owe him your life, so it's always a big problem, always hanging like a weight on you. If I would have to see my donor every day, I would have to be thanking him all

the time and that would be awful. I didn't want to see the face of the kidney seller, so that I would never have to think about him again. I paid for it. He accepted it. It's done, over. His kidney inside me belongs to me now, the same as if it were a cadaver kidney.

There are dimensions of family sacrifice, betrayal and co-ercion hidden within both forms of living donation, related and commercialized.

By transforming the 'gift' of an organ into a 'commodity,' the burden of debt to the giver is expunged. But as I describe next, family pressures and sacrifice are present even in the context of kidney buying and selling. In both instances—living-related and paid donation—weaker family members are recruited to sacrifice themselves in the interests of the family good.

In the watery slum of Banong Lupa, Manila, a site of active kidney selling, I stumbled on a troubling phenomenon. The obligation to sell a kidney to provide basic necessities for one's family initially fell on mature male heads of households. Over time, kidney selling became routine and perceived as a meritorious act of self-sacrifice, demonstrating the lengths to which a good husband and father would go to protect his family. On a return to Manila in 2003 as part of a documentary film team, I observed many more scarred bodies among young men and boys, even teenagers, who had lied about their age to be accepted as paid donors in public and private hospitals there. Sixteen-year-old Faustino was recruited by his maternal uncle, Ray Arcela, a former kidney seller. 'It's *your turn*', Uncle Ray told the boy reminding him that Faustino's father and his two older brothers had already sold a kidney. The $2000 earned per kidney never got these large families out of trouble. Similarly, Andreas was 17 when his mother begged him to sell a kidney so she could purchase the cases of beer, cokes and hard liquor she sold out of her shack. A good son, Andreas could not refuse his mother's request. Kidney selling had become a rite of passage among adolescents, and a kidney scar across the torso of a teenager was as common as a large tattoo. Just as tattoos signified membership in a youth subculture, the long scar across the torso symbolized *machismo*, courage and family loyalty, indicating the boy's attempt to support his parents.

While the social pathologies involved in kidney selling may seem distant from normative practices of altruistic kidney donation, I am suggesting that there are dimensions of family sacrifice, betrayal and coercion hidden within both forms of living donation, related and commercialized.

Old Bodies, Young Donors

My final scenario is, perhaps, the most controversial.

The number of kidneys transplanted in patients over 70 years has increased markedly over the past decade. As the US population ages, and as transplant has become routine, older patients are demanding the better quality of life that a transplant can bring. In the United States, with its highly *individualistic* notion of equality, there is a strong reluctance to disqualify the old from the benefits of transplant, and their physicians are reluctant to discourage them. Consequently, elderly patients are the fastest growing group requiring renal transplant. As of 1 November 2006, 10,628 patients over 65 are wait-listed for an organ. A hospital in Pennsylvania recently transplanted a kidney from a deceased donor into a 90-year-old patient. In some parts of Europe and the United States the demand has been partially offset by offering elderly patients older, sicker organs, euphemistically referred to as 'extended criteria' organs. While there are ethical quandaries in so doing, old-to-old organ transplants, expresses a kind of social justice and equity. From a purely social utilitarian perspective the practice enhances the longevity of younger organs reserved for 'younger' recipients.

Another solution is more troubling, an increase in living donation by adult children and grandchildren for their parents and grandparents. Of the 1,684 kidneys transplanted to patients over 65 in 2003, 513 were from living donors and 295 from adult children of the recipients. Children in their 30s, 40s and 50s gave kidneys to parents in their 60s and 70s. An ethnographic study by Sharon Kaufman at UC [University of California] San Francisco identified a subtle practice through which children were recruited by transplant professionals to donate to their elders. This practice violates a cultural norm in American society where it is not generally expected that children be unstintingly devoted to their parents, something that generations of immigrants from Europe were happy to leave behind. Rather, American parents are expected to give unstintingly to their children. Thus, statistics compiled by the kidney transplant registry in the 1970s show that within families mothers were the primary living-related organ donors, followed by fathers and siblings. Less than 1% of living donation was of children to their parents.

What has happened since that period? The current situation reflects the impact of the availability of extreme life-saving measures on family dynamics. As aging and death are increasingly viewed as the result of 'technological failures' rather than as human inevitability, older patients grasp for technological straws, and their physicians collude with them. Kaufman captures the moment in the following example. *Physician to a 71-year-old woman*: 'Getting you a live donor kidney would be a great thing. And the sooner the better. It could be five or six years if you wait for a cadaver donor'. Today, kidney patients are aware of the added value of a live over a dead donor. In some circles of patient activism, the preference for a 'fresh' kidney from a living donor is so strong that deceased donors are now viewed with distaste. 'A fresh live organ is the most *natural*, the best choice', a transplant recipient in New York City told me. A dapper gent in his 80s explained why he had chosen to travel for an illegal transplant with a (paid) young living donor from Romania:

> Why should I have to wait for a kidney from an accident, a kidney that was pinned under a car for many hours, then kept on ice for several hours. . . . That kidney is not going to be any good! Even worse, I could get the organ of an elderly person, or an alcoholic, or a person who died of a stroke. That kidney is all used up! It's much better to get a kidney from a healthy person.

My concerns are not with the medical risks of living donation but with the less visible social and familial conundrums it provokes.

While it is easy to distance oneself from the experience of transplant tourists who are willing to break the law to get what they want, the logic employed by some doctors and their elderly recipients is not dissimilar. Kaufman recorded the words of a physician to a 77-year-old man in California with heart disease: 'Realistically, *you will have to have someone donate you a kidney* if you ever want to get one'.

This 'quiet revolution' in kidney transplant raises many issues and is purchased at a great social cost, in the obligations felt by children to forfeit a 'spare' kidney for the elderly parents. Lungs and half livers are the next goalpost in sight.

Restoring a Social Ethic to Transplant

In the early days of transplant, living donation was the exception to a 'preferential option' for the brain dead donor. That initial ethical shudder, that hesitancy to take from the young and the healthy to rescue the old and the mortally ill is no longer an obstacle. While the medical benefits of living donation for the recipient and the psychological and spiritual benefits for the donors have been discussed I want to recover the discomfort in dipping too readily into the bodies of living donors. I am suggesting, if not a moratorium, a *slowing down* of the use of living donors, especially young ones. My concerns are not with the medical risks of living donation but with the less visible social and familial conundrums it provokes. These fall outside the view of transplant professionals and require the skills of the medical anthropologist and sociologist, who even more than bio-ethicists, are the real 'strangers at the bedside' of transplant patients.

Many specialists in the field would reply that deceased donors can never provide sufficient organs. They are unwilling, however, to examine the waiting list to see if futile cases cannot, in good faith, be removed and to establish age limits that would decrease the list by several thousand. Doing so, however, would put more pressure on living donors to rescue disqualified loved ones, and on very sick or very old patients to search for illegal transplants abroad, or to list patients online in a search unaccompanied by medical regulation or surveillance. Obviously, living and deceased donation impact each other and these two systems of procurement have to be considered conjointly.

Ethical solutions are not always palatable. Rather than find new ways to compensate or honor living donors we need to continue the struggle to increase deceased donation. While awaiting the results of stem cell engineering, the development of advanced mechanical kidneys and xenotransplant [across species], we ought to consider options that have worked elsewhere. Presumed consent, widespread in central Europe, preserves the value of organ transplant as a common social good in which no one is included or excluded on the basis of their ability to pay. Living donation, however, should be consigned to a back seat as an exceptional back-up to deceased donation.

10

Body Part Recipients Should Not Be Selected on Moral Grounds

Sally Satel

Sally Satel is a psychiatrist and the editor of When Altruism Isn't Enough: The Case for Compensating Kidney Donors.

When transplantable organs and medical advances are scarce, decisions must be made in regard to who receives these life-saving treatments. In 2008, media coverage of California gang members receiving organs and then later donating large sums of money to the University of California at Los Angeles (UCLA) medical center brought these concerns to light once again. In the 1960s kidney dialysis became an advanced practice, but the machines were expensive and scarce. So-called "God committees" were formed to choose who would receive such treatments. Although these committees were later disbanded, issues like those expressed in the California cases continue to plague the availability of transplantable organs.

According to a recent investigation by the *Los Angeles Times*, four members of the *yakuza*, the Japanese mafia, received liver transplants at the UCLA medical center between 2000 and 2004. Two of the four men later gave a $100,000 contribution to the medical center, prompting speculation that a cash promise got them bumped to the head of the transplant waiting list. The story suggested that this revelation could

Sally Satel, "The God Committee: Should Criminals Have Equal Access to Scarce Medical Treatments?" *Slate*, June 17, 2008. Reprinted with permission of the author.

"have a chilling effect on organ donation." That worry already seems well-founded. "I'd say kill the gang members and take their organs to give to law-abiding citizens," read one of the hundreds of hostile posts on the *Times'* Web site. "You're not getting mine!" said another. "I'm removing my name from the Donor list immediately." A third charged that *UCLA* actually stands for "Universally Corrupt Liver Auctioneers."

There was a time, however, when character did determine access to scarce treatment.

In an op-ed, UCLA tried to defend itself. Dr. Gerald S. Levey, dean of the David Geffen School of Medicine at the university, denied that the men had been whisked in for operations ahead of others. As for the public outcry surrounding the moral standing of the Japanese men, he said, "those who argue that criminals should not get transplants are on shaky ethical ground. Do we want to force caregivers to make a life-or-death decision based on whether a patient is a 'good' or 'bad' person?"

It's a perfect storm of ethical anxieties: good organs going to bad people; medical professionals (perhaps) on the take; and, not least, a shudder of xenophobia [fear or hatred of foreigners]. Levey is, of course, on entirely safe ground in arguing that physicians should not withhold vital treatment from their patients. But when resources are scarce—transplantable organs being the classic example—should some institution pass judgment when facts about a patient's criminality are known? No, says the United Network for Organ Sharing, which coordinates procurement and distribution of organs from the newly deceased. As Mark Fox, former head of the UNOS ethics committee, told me, "Once patients have been placed on the waiting list, the list itself is blind to whether you are a saint or sinner, a celebrity or a derelict."

Seattle's Swedish Hospital's "God Committee"

There was a time, however, when character did determine access to scarce treatment. In devising a way to select patients, physicians imagined that the public preferred to think of decision-makers as wise stewards of scarce resources. In 1962, Seattle's Swedish Hospital established what later came to be called the "God Committee." Formally known as the Admissions and Policy Committee of the Seattle Artificial Kidney Center at Swedish Hospital, its task was to decide which terminal patient would get access to scarce dialysis machines, or artificial kidneys, as they were called then.

The committee grew out of a medical breakthrough achieved by Dr. Belding Scribner of the University of Washington. He succeeded in converting acute dialysis (good for perhaps six weeks) into a chronic procedure that could last many years. At the time, 10,000 Americans were estimated to be dying from renal failure each year. Scribner's discovery made Seattle a center for the new field of nephrology [treatment of kidney diseases], and when the Artificial Kidney Center opened in the city in January 1962, it was the only dialysis center in the country. There were three treatment slots and about 60 patients in the surrounding area who needed them. Scribner argued that choosing among medically eligible candidates was not a clinical deliberation; it was a societal one. And, as such, the burden of choice should be shared by the public.

In the face of scarcity, choices need to be made.

The Seattle committee was composed of seven lay people—a lawyer, a minister, a housewife, a state government official, a banker, a labor leader, and a surgeon who served as a "doctor-citizen"—and was among the earliest instances, if not the first, of physicians bringing nonprofessionals into the realm of clinical decision-making. The members, all unpaid, insisted on anonymity. They considered the prospective patient's marital status, net worth, nature of occupation, extent of education, church attendance, number of dependents (the more kids or dependent relatives, the better the chance of being chosen), and potential to resume work. They struggled with the ultimate question of who should be saved: the person who contributes the most to society or the one whose death would impose the greatest burden on society, in the form of children left without care or resources.

In November 1962, *Life* magazine ran Shana Alexander's now-classic story about the committee. The article, "They Decide Who Lives, Who Dies," drew national attention to the drama playing out in Seattle. As Alexander showed, the members of the committee took their Solomonic [after king Solomon, requiring great wisdom] charge very seriously. "As human beings ourselves," one told her, "we rejected the idea instinctively, of classifying other human beings in pigeonholes, but we realized we had to narrow the field somehow." Thirty years later, Alexander gave a speech titled "Covering the God Committee," and from that point, the name stuck.

Critics of the God Committees

Critics of the God Committee charged that rationing by measure of human worth was an affront to the ideal of equality. But in the face of scarcity, choices need to be made. As the technology for dialysis spread across the country, other selection committees were established. But they were less explicit than the first Seattle effort had been about making judgments about human worth. "Physicians learned from Seattle to avoid the 'costs' of being highly visible in decision-making about who received treatment," says Richard A. Rettig, a political scientist who chronicled the social history of dialysis policy. They made their choices based on predictions of which patients would be able to adhere to the demands of dialysis treatment (strict diet, meticulous hygiene, and reliable attendance several times a week) and which were likely to return to a socially useful role.

This meant that the selection committees took nonmedical traits into account. For example, some tested IQ, personality, and the vocational skills of dialysis candidates. The Peter Bent Brigham dialysis program considered the likelihood of a return to productivity and cooperation with care. The Los Angeles County Dialysis Center screened for a group of medically, psychologically, and socially optimum candidates and then selected among them by lottery. The Cleveland Clinic allowed patients access to dialysis on a first-come, first-served basis and culled only if some proved unwilling or unable to cooperate once they had begun the therapy. Only a few centers explicitly disqualified candidates because of criminal records, spotty employment, or indigence. But the chances of being chosen if you fell into these categories were not good, because the traits in question suggested a lack of the material and emotional wherewithal to comply with the demands of lifelong dialysis treatment.

Soon, many of the God committees became demoralized at having to preside over so many deaths. By 1972, pressure from advocates and physician groups was strong enough to move Congress to establish universal funding for dialysis through Medicare. The supply of limited resources—dialysis machines and facilities—increased overnight. And the wrenching ethical dilemmas of allocation disappeared, along with the God committees intended to resolve them.

After decades of public education about organ donation, the gap between supply and demand grows ever wider.

The legacy of the Seattle committee lives on as a historic milestone, perhaps "the birth of bioethics," in the words of bioethicist Albert Jonsen. No one wants to return to the days of the character biopsy—judging a patient's social value—in deciding who gets access to rare treatments. But the UCLA story and others like it will continue to offend our sense of fairness as long as the nation's dire organ shortage persists. The only way to dispel the ethical quandaries that stem from rationing is to expand the pool of organs so that more people can receive lifesaving transplants.

So far, we have failed on this front. After decades of public education about organ donation, the gap between supply and demand grows ever wider. Last year, more than 6,000 people died waiting for an organ that never came. Out of desperation, some patients travel abroad for transplants. They do so with the sickening knowledge that their new kidneys or livers will come from a poor native exploited by brokers in the underground organ bazaars that flourish across the globe.

It is time for the federal government to acknowledge that altruistic giving has not produced enough organs. Repealing the ban on donor compensation would permit the federal or state governments to devise a safe, regulated system in which would-be donors are rewarded for giving an organ to the next stranger on the list. If only the organ shortage itself provoked as much outrage as the UCLA mobster transplants.

11

Traditions in Developing Countries Facilitate the Sale of Body Parts

Sabella Abidde

Sabella Abidde is a Nigerian journalist who writes about contemporary African issues.

The illegal trade of human body parts is a phenomenon that has occurred throughout human history and continues around the world. The use of human body parts differs by culture. In modern-day Nigeria, they are used primarily for magical rituals. Fake clinics and mortuaries have been set up to harvest organs from the near-dead and recently deceased. Dealers in body parts can make a significant living as organs are in demand around the world.

Those in the know know where to go in order to partake in such activity. Human sacrifice may come by way of beheading or burning or the victims buried alive.

Indeed, there are several rituals surrounding human sacrifice, all of which are beyond the scope of this treatise. Most human sacrifices are done for religious reasons—to appease or please deities and spirits. As horrendous as it sounds, human sacrifice is actually not a new phenomenon: it has been taking place from the beginning of time in all cultures through all ages and civilizations.

The Mayans and the Aztecs, the Phoenicians, Carthaginians, Chinese, Japanese, Indians, and others all engaged in hu-

Sabella Abidde, "Buying and Selling Human Body Parts in Nigeria," Ocnus.Net, May 3, 2007. Reproduced by permission of the author.

man sacrifice. And indeed, the Bible holds a sumptuous account of human sacrifices. The uninformed and the prejudiced in modern times are wont to think that human sacrifice originated, and lives on in Africa (they point to Africa when they have something bad and unpalatable to say about humanity).

Magical Purposes

But beyond human sacrifice for religious purposes are the procuring, buying, and selling of human cadavers and body parts for magical and scientific reasons. It doesn't matter what part of the world you are, there is a market nearby for buyers and sellers. Whatever you want and however you want it, they are all available for a price. In China it is alleged that prisoners and the executed are sometimes harvested for their body parts. In India, some very poor and very miserable people willingly sell body parts, i.e. kidneys, just to make ends meet. However, in Britain and Germany, the US, Canada, Australia and France and other countries, body parts are harvested for scientific reasons—all for high prices.

In today's Nigeria body parts are sold and bought mostly for fetish and magical reasons. And most of the originating markets for body parts are to be found in the western and eastern part of the country; still, there is almost no part of the country where one couldn't find whatever part one was interested in. Even so, there are specific ethnic groups where it is culturally and religiously forbidden to engage in human sacrifice and or to trade in or violate dead bodies, i.e. the Ijaw ethnic group in the Niger Delta region of Nigeria.

Because of the activities of body raiders and body snatchers, some families have taken to desperate measures.

And indeed, there are people who believe that money and fame and good fortune can be acquired if certain parts of the human anatomy are consumed or sacrificed; there is the belief that supernatural commands can only be effected if certain body parts are altered. Legends abound about market women who use body parts as part of their trading strategy. It could be true or perhaps mere fabrication, but there is the story of a popular pepper soup joint in Port Harcourt, and others in Lagos, Aba, and Akure where it is alleged that the owners uses bits and pieces of human liver and human heart as spices.

Body Raiders and Body Snatchers

You ought to know that if your loved one suddenly and inexplicably disappears and has not been seen or heard from for more than 30 days, it is possible he or she has fallen victim to body raiders and body snatchers. There was a time in Lagos and Ibadan when the *Gbomo Gbomo* phenomenon was very common. And indeed, all over Nigeria people disappear every single day not to be seen alive again. In some instances, the corpse may be seen, but without the vital body organs. To be sure, there are some parts of Nigeria you don't venture into without adequate security; there are alleys you just don't walk into without necessary protection. You just don't do it. If your vehicles break down in the wrong part of town or if you take the wrong turn, you just might fall into the hands of body raiders and body snatchers.

There are fake clinics and mortuaries doubling as slaughterhouses. In some parts of Nigeria, it is neither uncommon nor surprising for corpses to disappear from mortuaries, cemeteries, hospital beds and funeral homes. One really has to be vigilant; otherwise, the body of a loved one will disappear even before the body is cold and stiff. A friend of a friend told of how cemeteries are being raided—not just for jewelries and other saleable items—but mostly for body parts. It's been said that the liver, tongue, brain, kidney, lungs, and the eyes are much wanted; but the most priced parts are the breasts, private parts, and the heart—all of which can be bought in some not so discreet open markets the way beef and chicken and goats are sold and bought.

Because of the activities of body raiders and body snatchers, some families have taken to desperate measures: if the bodies are to be interned in the general cemetery, the burial is done almost in secrecy or the bodies are entombed in "bomb shelters." Some have even taken to burying the dead inside the deceased compound or private cemeteries. You don't want to bury your loved one only to find out 24–72 hours later that his or her body has been harvested. Famous, rich and popular Nigerians are especially at risk because of the belief that their organs will allow for the same fortune the deceased had while alive.

In countries where body parts are used for scientific purposes, here is the going rate for some parts (which are subject to the laws of demand and supply and other market forces): $3000 for a cornea; $80 for a patch of skin; $2000 for a kidney; a torso in good condition is almost $5,000; a spine $3,500; and a knee $650. A box of fingernails and toenails goes for as much as $5,000. But really, no part of the human body is a complete waste. And in fact, aborted babies are also sold; but the late-term aborted babies are much in demand. In most western countries, a trader in body parts can make upward of $500,000 a year.

But unfortunately, body parts are almost free in Nigeria and other African countries as snatchers and harvesters are primarily concerned with voodoo and magical use of such organs.

12

Traditional Beliefs Must Be Overcome to Facilitate Organ Donation

Leslie Susser with Robert Berman

Leslie Susser is the diplomatic correspondent for the Jerusalem Report *and also reports for the* Jewish Journal.

Prohibiting the sale of organs not only results in many needless deaths, it also discriminates against the poor. Although most opponents of a legalized organ trade cite the exploitation of impoverished peoples as a primary reason for prohibition, in reality poor people suffer from these outdated laws because only the rich can afford to purchase black market organs. In addition, if selling organs was made legal, the risks of complications from poorly done operations would be lessened. Jewish people, especially, should consider donating their organs because it is in keeping with Jewish law, or halakhah.

The death of 38-year-old Oren Azarya at Beilinson Hospital in Petah Tikvah [Israel] on September 12, [2005], a few hours after undergoing surgery to remove a kidney he was donating for a transplant, raises a number of acute ethical dilemmas: Should live donors be encouraged to donate organs despite the risks involved? Should donors be paid? How should the severe shortage of organs for lifesaving transplants worldwide be addressed? What does Jewish law, *halakhah*, say?

Azarya may have died because he was being illegally paid for the organ. He insisted on going through with the procedure, although a previous attempt to remove the kidney was aborted when he showed signs of weakness. Robert Berman, founder and director of the New York-based Halachic Organ Donor Society [HODS], insists that the problem is not payment for organs, but the fact that such payments today are illegal. Indeed, he argues that legalizing payment to live donors for their organs would actually make organ donations safer and reduce the imbalance between supply and demand.

Berman set up HODS three and a half years ago to convince Jews that *halakhah* not only allows organ donation, but considers it a *mitzvah* [an act of human kindness]. Since then he has managed to persuade about 2,000 Orthodox Jews, including over 100 rabbis, to carry organ donor cards. Last September HODS, a strategic partner with the Israel Transplant Center, located Eric Swim, the Kansas man whose kidney donation saved the life of 10-year-old Moshiko Sharon of Moshav Hodayah [Israeli settlement]. In a telephone conversation from New York, Berman maintains that the real problem is that people are dying for lack of organs available for lifesaving transplants.

The Jerusalem Report: Why do you think legalizing the sale of organs would help?

Robert Berman: First of all, there's the simple question of supply and demand. One of the most powerful ways of increasing supply is by giving people money and incentivizing them to donate.

Secondly, the illegal purchase of organs today is similar to the abortions of yesteryear. Even though abortions were illegal, that didn't mean they stopped. They were carried out in dark rooms with coat-hangers, and people died. That's the equivalent of what's going on today with organs.

TJR: How rife is the illegal trade in human organs?

RB: Israeli doctors are arrested every year in places like China, Turkey, Bolivia and South Africa for doing this. And it's going to continue, because people's lives are on the line.

Who's to say what you or I would do if we needed a kidney and our only option was to purchase one illegally? It's hypocritical to forbid the purchasing of organs in the name of higher ethics, when it results in people dying.

TJR: How might legalization of payment have helped in Azarya's case?

RB: The fact that the donor who died in Israel was paid for his kidney did not cause him to die. But because the payment was illegal, he may have hidden details of his prior condition so he could go ahead and get the money. If payment were legalized, there would be a lot of people lining up to donate kidneys, and doctors could do proper medical checks and screenings and select only people in perfect health. They would have many more donors to choose from, and they would select only the healthiest people.

TJR: What does *halakhah* say about paying for organs?

RB: Three former chief rabbis have ruled that getting paid for an organ is not unethical. They argue that saving life is a good deed, and if you get paid for it, that doesn't diminish the ethical quality of the deed. If a doctor resuscitates me and saves my life in the emergency ward, we wouldn't say his act is any less ethical because he gets a paycheck.

Buying kidneys is only morally odious to those who don't need them to live.

TJR: Wouldn't it be a case of wealthy would-be recipients buying body parts from the less well-off?

RB: If a poor person can't afford to put his kids through school or pay the rent, and they decide they want to sell their kidney, they should be allowed to do it. At the moment, because it's illegal, the middlemen pick up most of the money.

Ironically, the ban on purchasing organs also allows for discrimination against the poor. Because of the people who need kidneys, only the wealthy can afford to buy them on the black market. It is the poor who can't and die. Some people find it objectionable to sell human organs because it makes a commodity of the human body. But that already exists. Men sell sperm, women sell eggs and hair, and even rent out their wombs. And it's not the upper class that is doing this, it's the lower class. Yet people aren't screaming it's unethical. Buying kidneys is only morally odious to those who don't need them to live.

TJR: What about the risk to live donors?

RB: The risk with regard to kidneys is medically acceptable. The risk of the surgery is so small that the medical profession allows a person to walk into a clinic and altruistically donate his kidney for no money. Even assuming there is an element of risk, that doesn't make organ donations unethical. Society often offers incentives to people who take risks, and it compensates them. People who take risks building bridges and tunnels, firemen, bomb disposal experts, journalists in war zones all get hazard pay.

Organizations to Contact

The editors have composed the following list of organizations concerned with the issues debated in this book. The descriptions are derived from materials provided by the organizations. All have publications or information available for interested readers. The list was compiled on the date of publication of the present volume; the information provided here may change. Be aware that many organizations take several weeks or longer to respond to inquiries, so allow as much time as possible.

American Society of Transplant Surgeons (ASTS)
2461 South Clark Street, Suite 640, Arlington, VA   22202
(703) 414-7870 • fax: (703) 414-7874
Web site: www.asts.org

The ASTS is comprised of over nearly 1,200 transplant surgeons, physicians, and scientists who are dedicated to education and research in all aspects of organ donation and transplantation. The ASTS seeks to advance the practice of transplantation and to guide those who make policy decisions that influence transplantation. Several of the organization's position statements focus on the ethics of donor compensation, including "Health Insurance as Incentive for Living Kidney Donation" and "Directed Donation and Solicitation of Donor Organs."

American Society of Transplantation (AST)
15000 Commerce Parkway, Suite C, Mt. Laurel, NJ   08054
(856) 439-9986 • fax: (856) 439-9982
e-mail: ast@ahint.com
Web site: www.a-s-t.org

Founded in 1982, the AST is an international organization of transplant professionals aimed at advancing the field of transplantation. Through awareness campaigns and public programs, the AST promotes current transplantation research and patient advocacy methods. The AST regularly publishes research in several publications, including *Conversations in Transplantation* and the *American Journal of Transplantation*.

Amnesty International
5 Penn Plaza, 14th Floor, New York, NY   10001
(212) 807-8400 • fax: (212) 463-9193
e-mail: admin-us@aiusa.org
Web site: www.amnestyusa.org

Amnesty International is a worldwide movement of people who campaign for internationally recognized human rights. By providing articles, publications, pamphlets, and video media, the organization seeks to educate people about all human rights violations and call people to action. Amnesty International prints regular reports about the worldwide organ trade, including "Execution Vans, Organ Harvesting—Business as Usual in China."

Global Organization for Donation (GOOD)
P.O. Box 52757, Tulsa, OK   74105
(918) 605-1994 • fax: (918) 745-6637
e-mail: info@global-good.org
Web site: www.global-good.org

GOOD is a nonprofit organization dedicated to saving lives; raising awareness for organ, eye, and tissue donation; correcting misconceptions about donation, and increasing the number of people willing to donate life. GOOD's "Circle of Life" newspaper campaign helps people understand more about the donation process, gives donor and recipient families a way to tell their important stories about donation and provides newspapers, organ procurement organizations and funeral homes the information they need to become participating partners. In addition, GOOD also issues press releases about facts and myths regarding the ethics of organ donation, including compensation for organs.

HumanTrafficking.org
1825 Connecticut Ave., NW, Washington, DC 20009-5721
(202) 884-8916
e-mail: director@humantrafficking.org
Web site: www.humantrafficking.org

The purpose of this Web site is to bring government and non-government organizations in East Asia and the Pacific together to cooperate and learn from each other's experiences in their efforts to combat human trafficking. The site contains country-specific information, such as national laws and action plans, and descriptions of various organizations' activities worldwide. In addition to a library of publications on human trafficking in general, a special section of the Web site focuses on the trafficking of human organs.

The International Association for Organ Donation (IAOD)
P.O. Box 545, Dearborn, MI 48121
(313) 745-2379
Web site: www.iaod.org

Since the organization's inception in 1999, the IAOD has been active in organ, tissue, and bone marrow donations. IAOD primarily targets the largest ethnic communities most affected by the disparity between donors and recipients, including the Arab/Chaldean, African, Asian, and Hispanic American communities. In addition to telethons and other public awareness campaigns, the IAOD also educates the public with facts sheets and brochures.

National Kidney Foundation (NKF)
30 East 33rd Street, New York, NY 10016
(800) 622-9010 • fax: (212) 689-9261
Web site: www.kidney.org

The National Kidney Foundation, a major voluntary nonprofit health organization, is dedicated to preventing kidney and urinary tract diseases, improving the health and well-being of individuals and families affected by kidney disease, and increasing the availability of all organs for transplantation. Through its more than 50 local offices nationwide, the NKF provides vital patient and community services, conducts extensive public and professional education, advocates for patients through legislative action, and supports kidney research to identify new treatments. NKF regularly publishes reports and position statements, many of which have focused on its opposition to the buying and selling of human organs.

OrganSelling.com
BSTWR E1407, University of Pittsburgh
Pittsburgh, PA   15260
(412) 648-9443
e-mail: htk@pitt.edu
Web site: www.organselling.com

OrganSelling.com is a Web site devoted to collecting information about establishing a worldwide, free market organ trade in which donors would be compensated for their organs. In addition to a statement of purpose, the site also offers links to the most recent research done on donor compensation, a patient stories section, and a forum for visitors to discussion organ transplantation issues.

Organs Watch Berkeley
232 Kroeber Hall, University of California, Berkeley
Berkeley, CA   94720
e-mail: orgwatch@uclink4.berkeley.edu
Web site: http://sunsite.berkeley.edu/biotech/organswatch

Organs Watch Berkeley is a nonprofit organization that investigates and documents the trafficking of human organs and violations of international laws and human rights. Organs Watch researchers track down rumors, document cases of black-market organ sales, and follow individual countries' laws pertaining to organ harvesting and transplantation. The organization's many publications include "The Global Traffic in Organs" and "Truth and Rumor on the Organ Trail."

Transplant Recipients International Organization (TRIO)
2100 M Street, NW, #170-353, Washington, DC 20037-1233
(800) TRIO-386
e-mail: info@trioweb.org
Web site: www.trioweb.org

TRIO is a nonprofit international organization committed to improving the quality of lives touched by transplantation through support, advocacy, education, and awareness. One of its major efforts involves taking the concerns and needs that affect the welfare of transplant candidates, recipients, and their families to federal, state, and local government bodies. In addition to regularly publishing the *Lifelines* newsletter, TRIO also posts position statements about organ donation, including, "Your Choice First! A Presumed Consent Policy for Organ Donation" and "The Trouble with: 1—Paying Cash for Organs; 2—Presumed Consent; 3—Putting Signed-up Donors at the Head of the List."

United Network for Organ Sharing (UNOS)
P.O. Box 2484, Richmond, VA 23218
(888) 894-6361
e-mail: crowmg@unos.org
Web site: www.unos.org

Located in Richmond, Virginia, UNOS is a nonprofit, scientific and educational organization that administers the nation's only Organ Procurement and Transplantation Network, established by the U.S. Congress in 1984. UNOS's mission is to advance organ availability and transplantation by uniting and supporting communities for the benefit of patients through education, technology, and policy development. In addition to fact sheets and patient brochures, UNOS offers a number of publications through its Web site, including "Ethics of Organ Donation From Condemned Prisoners" and "Financial Incentives for Organ Donation."

World Health Organization (WHO)
Avenue Appia 20, Geneva 27   1211
  Switzerland
41-22-791-21-11 • fax: 41-22-791-31-11
e-mail: info@who.int
Web site: www.who.int

WHO is the directing and coordinating authority for health within the United Nations system. It is responsible for providing leadership on global health matters, shaping the health research agenda, setting norms and standards, articulating evidence-based policy options, providing technical support to countries, and monitoring and assessing health trends. Several of its many investigative reports have focused on the buying and selling of human organs, including "The State of the International Organ Trade" and "Human Organ and Tissue Transplantation."

Bibliography

Books

John Candlish   *Hawking Spleens, Selling Genes: The Human Body and the Laws of Property*. Kota Samarahan: Universiti Malaysia Sarawak, 2006.

Annie Cheney   *Body Brokers: Inside America's Underground Trade in Human Remains*. New York: Broadway Books, 2007.

Mark J. Cherry   *Kidney for Sale by Owner: Human Organs, Transplantation, and the Market*. Washington, DC: Georgetown University Press, 2005.

Stephen Cullenberg and Prasanta K. Pattanaik, eds.   *Globalization, Culture, and the Limits of the Market: Essays in Economics and Philosophy*. New York: Oxford University Press, 2004.

Decision Resources   *The SAGE Handbook of Healthcare: Global Policies, Business Opportunities, Scientific Developments*. London: SAGE, 2008.

Donna Dickenson   *Property in the Body: Feminist Perspectives*. New York: Cambridge University Press, 2007.

Cécile Fabre   *Whose Body Is It Anyway?: Justice and the Integrity of the Person*. New York: Oxford University Press, 2006.

Francis Godwyll
and So Young
Kang, eds.

Poverty, Education, and Development.
New York: Nova Science, 2008.

Michele Goodwin

*Black Markets: The Supply and
Demand of Body Parts.* New York:
Cambridge University Press, 2006.

Kieran Healy

*Last Best Gifts: Altruism and the
Market for Human Blood and Organs.*
Chicago: University of Chicago Press,
2006.

Charles C.
Hinkley II

*Moral Conflicts of Organ Retrieval: A
Case for Constructive Pluralism.* New
York: Rodopi, 2005.

Paul Kurtz, ed.

*Science and Ethics: Can Science Help
Us Make Wise Moral Judgments?*
Amherst, NY: Prometheus Books,
2007.

David Matas and
David Kilgour

*Bloody Harvest: Revised Report into
Allegations of Organ Harvesting of
Falun Gong Practitioners in China.*
Washington, DC: Coalition to
Investigate the Persecution of the
Falun Gong in China, 2007.

Remigius N.
Nwabueze

*Biotechnology and the Challenge of
Property: Property Rights in Dead
Bodies, Body Parts, and Genetic
Information.* Burlington, VT: Ashgate,
2007.

David Petechuk

Organ Transplantation. Westport, CT:
Greenwood Press, 2006.

Rosamond Rhodes, Leslie P. Francis, and Anita Silvers, eds.

The Blackwell Guide to Medical Ethics. Malden, MA: Blackwell, 2007.

Alan Rubenstein

On the Body and Transplantation: Philosophical and Legal Context. Washington, DC: President's Council on Bioethics, 2007.

David Steinberg, ed.

Biomedical Ethics: A Multidisciplinary Approach to Moral Issues in Medicine and Biology. Hanover, NH: University Press of New England, 2007.

James Stacey Taylor

Stakes and Kidneys: Why Markets in Human Body Parts Are Morally Imperative. Burlington, VT: Ashgate, 2005.

Stuart J. Youngner, Martha W. Anderson, and Renie Schapiro, eds.

Transplanting Human Tissue: Ethics, Policy, and Practice. New York: Oxford University Press, 2004.

Periodicals

Karen Aho

"Selling Body Parts for Cash," MSN Money, 2009.

Cameron Ainsworth-Vincze

"Were Kosovo Patients Slain for Organs?" *Maclean's*, December 1, 2008.

Tarif Bakdash
and Nancy
Scheper-Hughes

"Is It Ethical for Patients with Renal
Disease to Purchase Kidneys from
the World's Poor?" *PLoS Medicine* 3,
no. 10, October 2006.

Jennifer S. Bard

"Black Markets: The Supply and
Demand of Body Parts," *Journal of
Health Politics, Policy and Law* 33, no.
1, February 2008.

Randy Barrett

"Kidneys R Us," *National Journal*,
April 18, 2008.

*Cambridge
Quarterly of
Healthcare Ethics*

"Commercial Organ Transplantation
in the Philippines," vol. 18, no. 2,
April 2009.

Marc Champion
and Gabriel Kahn

"Horrors Alleged in Kosovo," *Wall
Street Journal*, April 14, 2008.

Anuj Chopra

"Harvesting Kidneys from the Poor
for Rich Patients," *U.S. News & World
Report*, February 18, 2008.

Carlos H. Conde

"The Philippines: No More Kidneys
for Foreigners, Government Decrees,"
New York Times, April 30, 2008.

Economist

"Psst, Wanna Buy a Kidney?"
November 16, 2006.

Eli A. Friedman
and Amy L.
Friedman

"Reassessing Marketing of Kidneys
from the 2008 Perspective," *Blood
Purification* 27, no. 1, January 2009.

Anne Griffin

"Kidneys on Demand," *British
Medical Journal* 334, no. 7295, March
31, 2007.

Alexander   "China in Forefront in Human Parts
Hermijlin   Harvesting," *New York Amsterdam
News*, May 10, 2007.

Kerry Howley   "Who Owns Your Body Parts?"
Reason, March 2007.

Jeneen Interlandi "Not Just Urban Legend," *Newsweek*,
January 19, 2009.

Jane's   "Organ Trafficking: A Fast-Expanding
Information   Black Market," March 5, 2008.
Group

Mohammed I.   "Organ Trading in Jordan: Bad News,
Khalili   Good News," *Politics and the Life
Sciences* 26, no. 1, March 2007.

Lancet   "Not for Sale at Any Price," April 18,
2006.

Ana Lita   "The Dark Side of Organ
Transplantation," *Humanist*,
March/April 2008.

Laura Meckler   "Kidney Shortage Inspires a Radical
Idea: Organ Sales," *Wall Street
Journal*, November 13, 2007.

Gilbert   "The Giving and Taking of Organs,"
Meilaender   *First Things: A Monthly Journal of
Religion and Public Life*, no. 181,
March 2008.

Silke Meyer   "Trafficking in Human Organs in
Europe: A Myth or an Actual
Threat?" *European Journal of Crime,
Criminal Law, and Criminal Justice*
14, no. 2, 2006.

Richard C. Morais   "Desperate Arrangements," *Forbes*, January 29, 2007.

New Scientist   "Governments Urged to Crack Down on Transplant Tourism," July 21, 2008.

New York Times Magazine   "Flesh Trade," July 23, 2006.

Newsweek   "Organ Trafficking Is Real, and Booming," January 19, 2009.

Luc Noël   "Current Concerns in Transplantation," *Bulletin of the World Health Organization*, December 2007.

Bojan Pancevski   "Bulgarian Hospital Admits Role in Illegal Transplants," *Lancet*, February 11, 2006.

Randall Patterson   "The Organ Grinder," *New York*, October 16, 2006.

Mohammad A. Rai and Omer Afzal   "Organs in the Bazaar: The End of the Beginning?" *Politics and the Life Sciences*, March 2007.

Bernardo Rodriguez-Iturbe   "Organ Trafficking: A Time for Action," *Kidney International* 74, no. 7, October 2008.

Sandy Sand   "Selling Body Parts to Make Ends Meet: A Sign of the Times," *Digital Journal*, February 25, 2009.

Sally Satel   "Why We Need a Market for Human Organs," *Wall Street Journal*, May 16, 2008.

Jeremy Shearmur   "The Real Body Shop, Part Two: Spare Parts," *Policy* 24, no. 1, Autumn 2008.

John Stossel   "Hostility to Free Markets Can Cost Lives," *Human Events*, January 21, 2008.

Frank Thomas   "Rent-a-Womb Is Where Market Logic Leads," *Wall Street Journal*, December 10, 2008.

Emily Waltz   "News Feature: The Body Snatchers," *Nature Medicine*, May 2006.

Jonathan Watts   "China Introduces New Rules to Deter Human Organ Trade," *Lancet*, June 9, 2007.

Stephen Wigmore   "Are China's Prisoners Being Killed to Order?" *Times Higher Education Supplement*, May 19, 2006.

John Zarocostas   "UN Calls for Tougher Rules to Prevent Sale of Children's Organs," *British Medical Journal* 334, no. 7295, March 31, 2007.

Index